Resources for Learning Mentors

A Lucky Duck Book

Paul Chapman Publishing
A SAGE Publications Company
1 Oliver's Yard
55 City Road
London EC1Y 1SP

SAGE Publications Inc.
2455 Teller Road
Thousand Oaks, California 91320

SAGE Publications India Pvt Ltd
B1/I 1 Mohan Cooperative Industrial Area
Mathura Road, New Delhi 110 044
India

SAGE Publications Asia-Pacific Pte Ltd
33 Pekin Street #02-01
Far East Square
Singapore 048763

www.luckyduck.co.uk

Commissioning Editor: Barbara Maines
Editorial: Sarah Lynch
Designer: Helen Weller

Library of Congress Control Number 2006938969
A catalogue record for this book is available from the British Library
ISBN 978-1-4129-3089-5

Printed on paper from sustainable resources
Printed in India at Replika Pvt Ltd

Resources for Learning Mentors

Group Work Activities for Working with:

Vulnerable Children

White Working Class Boys

Teenage Girls

**and a Course to Promote
Mental Health and Wellbeing**

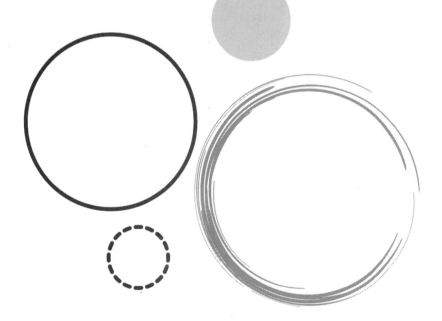

Pamela Allen

P·C·P
Paul Chapman
Publishing

Contents

Acknowledgements

I would like to thank the Interim Accommodation Sites staff in Sheffield, UK for allowing me to develop resources in collaboration with them. The work with vulnerable children has been challenging and fun. The willingness and passion from the workers at the site to improve the emotional climate for the young people they work with was humbling. I would like to thank Matt Scrivens, the homeless children's development worker, for supporting this pilot in his centre, in particular, his endless energy and commitment for wanting to get the resources right so that they could be used confidently in an informal play environment, was inspirational. Thanks to Raj and Sara, the play workers who tolerated us interrupting their normal play session and who provided honest and open feedback in the evaluation of the programme, and Peter Eggington, who has supported the staff to think creatively. Thanks also to Bea Kay who got me involved and helped me to pilot these materials.

Most importantly, I would like to thank the young people themselves who were living on the interim accommodation site during late 2004 and the beginning of 2005 and to the young people who took part in the school based programmes. They participated and engaged in the activities with great zest and gave feedback that was honest and direct. This brought to life the programmes, helped us to generate new ideas and to learn from our mistakes. Thank you all for being interested and having a go.

I would also like to thank the schools in Sheffield, especially the Learning Mentors who have collaborated with me in piloting resilience building groupwork programmes for children and young people in their schools. Particular thanks go to Parkwood School, Fir Vale School, Yewlands School, Chaucer School, (especially Marissa Palmer for co-facilitating the boys' group), Richard Hunt, Dianne Bradshaw and Cathy Charles who supported the running of the boys' group, Vicki Ransome and Rebecca Allard who collaborated with me in developing the girls' programme and Liz Jaques, who supported me running a girls' group.

I would also like to thank my colleagues in Child and Adolescent Mental Health Services in Sheffield who have supported me. Finally I would like to thank my family – my husband who supports and encourages me in all my work and my two children who inspire me to always want the best for other young people I meet.

Pam Allen

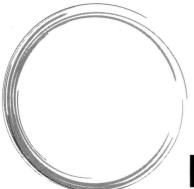

Foreword

I am very pleased to be able to write the foreword for this set of comprehensive, well thought-through and evaluated group work programmes. They are written on the premise that by building resilience, promoting a child's sense of self-worth or esteem and increasing emotional literacy, mental health can be improved or the impact of problems diminished. Various research has found that preventative or promotion programmes need to be focused on particular risk factors in order to be most effective, which these resources are.

Children's and young people's behaviour is often responded to negatively and negatively labelled without a consideration of the risk and resilience factors that may be in place for that individual. This pack of resources gives a reminder to think about these factors and provides materials to promote resilience. Although some programmes are targeted at particular groups, many of the group exercises can be used with all young people as a universal intervention.

The materials are very thorough and guide the reader from an introduction to the programme through to the use and importance of evaluation. I would therefore recommend following the programmes as they are written. They can be used in suitable ready-made group settings, such as within PSHE, or for groups that are set up specifically for this purpose.

The resources are compatible with all the major policy drivers for children and young people, most of which now recognise the importance of mental health promotion and problem prevention and the links with other aspects of a child's life. *Every Child Matters: Change for Children* (ECM) (2004) and the *National Service Framework for Children, Young People and Maternity Services* (NSF) (Department of Health and Department for Education and Skills, 2004) work alongside one another, mental health contributing to all the ECM standards but most obviously to the Be Healthy Standard. Standard 9 of the NSF – the Mental Health and Psychological Wellbeing of Children and Young People – states that all children should have access to supportive environments, and that there should be specific activities such as the provision of education to increase awareness of mental health issues, and that support should be provided for those with particular needs. These materials cover these aspects of mental health promotion and problem prevention.

Standard 9 also reminds us that the provision of early intervention may make a significant difference to children and their parents or carers, which is reiterated in Removing Barriers to Achievement: SEN Strategy (2004). This ensures that the link between good mental health and achievement are understood. These links are also clear within the National Healthy Schools Standard agenda and the Social and Emotional Aspects of Learning (SEAL) (DfES, 2005) which Mark Heaton has commented on in the foreword of the Healthy Minds chapter of this resource. Ofsted have also recognised that schools have a vital role to play in promoting children's mental health and in the early identification and prevention of mental health problems.

People who are mentally healthy also make healthier choices about their physical health as well as being more physically healthy, an idea incorporated into The Public Health White Paper – *Choosing Health; Making Healthy Choices Easier* (2006). The European Green Paper *Improving the Mental Health of the Population: Towards A Strategy on Mental Health for the European Union* supports early intervention very clearly:

> as mental health is strongly determined during the first few years of life, promoting mental health in children and adolescents is an investment for the future.

Overall, with the significant raise in the prevalence of psychosocial disorders (depression, eating disorders, substance misuse, suicide and suicidal behaviour and conduct disorders) in young people between the ages of 12 and 26 in Western developed countries since the end of the Second World War (Rutter and Smith, 1995) and the acknowledgement that mental health problems in children and young people are associated with educational failure, family disruption, disability, offending and anti-social behaviour, it is in the interests of all agencies to work towards promoting mental health and prevention of problems. If they are not addressed it can lead to more distress for the child and their families and carers, and may continue into adult life and affect the next generation. With this in mind, these materials are to be welcomed as a resource for good practice for Learning Mentors.

Jane Sedgewick

CAMHS Regional Development Worker (Yorkshire and the Humber),
National CAMHS Support Service, part of the Care Services Improvement Partnership.

Introduction – Planning the Programmes

Working within a prevention and promotion field of Child and Adolescent Mental Health for the last six years has influenced the planning of the programmes and ideas behind them.

Child and Adolescent Mental Health Services in Sheffield have been supportive in allowing a number of workers to focus on the promotion of mental and emotional wellbeing. This has led to work being developed both universally and targeted at vulnerable groups. The work we undertake has three main tenets: capacity building, building resilience and addressing the needs of at-risk groups.

Focusing on risk and resilience enables people to recognise what they are already doing to promote mental health, and to identify additional things they could do.

Risk and resilience factors can be divided into three spheres – those relating to the individual, those relating to the family and those relating to the community. The main factors are set out in Table 1.

Table 1 (DfES 2001)

Resilience factors	Risk factors
Within the child	**Within the child**
secure early relationships	academic failure
being female	genetic influences
higher intelligence	low IQ and learning disability
easy temperament when an infant	difficult temperament
positive attitude	specific developmental delay
problem-solving approach	physical illness, especially if chronic or neurological
good communication skills	communication difficulty
planner, belief in control	low self-esteem
humour	
religious faith	
capacity to reflect	
Within the family	**Within the family**
one good parent-child relationship	overt parental conflict
affection	family breakdown
clear, firm and consistent discipline	inconsistent, unclear discipline
support for education	failure to adapt to child's changing developmental needs
supportive long-term relationship	hostile and rejecting relationships
absence of severe discord	abuse
	parental psychiatric illness
	parental criminality
	alcoholism
	personality disorder
	death and loss
Within the community	**Within the community**
high standard of living	socio-economic disadvantage
good housing	homelessness
wider supportive networks	disaster
high morale school with positive policies for behaviour, attitudes and anti-bullying	discrimination
range of sport and leisure activities	other significant life events
schools with strong academic and non-academic opportunities	

Using a risk and resilience framework gives a way of thinking about mental health promotion, which makes it clear that frontline workers can play their part in supporting positive emotional wellbeing.

> The development of resilience, emotional intelligence and social competencies in young people is not only linked to long term occupational and life success but is also associated with the prevention of substance abuse, violence and suicide. (Fuller, 2001)

Many factors contribute to developing resilience but having supportive and caring relationships, both within and outside of the family, is a key factor. Fuller suggests that resilience depends on a sense of 'connectedness, belonging and empathy with others' and this sense of belonging determines the development of our morals such as 'honesty, altruism and caring' (2001). While relationships play an important role at all stages of development, it is a child's earliest relationships with an attachment figure that lay the foundations for future development.

A secure attachment in infancy leads to healthy, competent development in later years. This early relationship with a caregiver becomes a prototype for interactions and relationships a child will have later in life. Manning (2002) suggests that childhood attachment styles and the outcomes we have in adulthood can be mediated by developing, 'interpersonal competencies such as empathy, self-disclosure, and collaborative approaches to conflict, and of attitudes such as self-efficacy and social interest.' (Manning, 2002)

Secure attachment can therefore predispose young people to having more positive outcomes in competencies, satisfaction and greater social involvement. However, life experiences or interventions can also help develop social competence and responsibility. (Manning, 2002)

Other factors associated with resilience include:

▸ the capacity to make realistic plans and take steps to carry them out

▸ a positive view of yourself and confidence in your strengths and abilities

▸ skills in communication and problem-solving

▸ the capacity to manage strong feelings and impulses.

All of these skills can be learnt and developed. If a child learns to develop strategies of coping that are emotionally literate, positive and realistic then these will become lifetime habits (Goleman, 1995). Resilience is not a trait that people either have or do not have. It involves behaviours, thoughts, and actions that can be learned and developed in anyone.

At an individual level a key resilience factor that can be developed and nurtured, is self-esteem, or a sense of self-worth. This comes from feeling valued as an individual, with strengths recognised and celebrated, and effort appreciated. 'Self-esteem consists of global self-esteem (how good you feel about yourself as a person) and specific self-esteem (how capable you feel you are in accomplishing tasks)' (Fuller, 2001). Fuller also suggests that not all people with high self-esteem are resilient because resilience has a number of dimensions that are not all in an individual's control. This means that schools, communities and families all need to be involved and develop strategies which promote resilience.

The activities within these programmes are designed so that adults can promote children's and young people's sense of self-worth and that children and young people can celebrate their creative achievements, which can help them feel safe and valued.

Emotional literacy, sometimes called emotional intelligence, is another factor that increases resilience. Emotional regulation is one of the most essential components of mental health. The development of emotional regulation is influenced by parenting, schooling, psycho-educational and socialising opportunities.

Emotional literacy is a term encompassing the ability to recognise, reflect on and manage one's own emotions, the ability to recognise and empathise with others' emotions, and the ability to use these to form and maintain meaningful relationships and solve social and emotional problems. Like self-esteem, emotional literacy is something children acquire through their interactions with others, through the role models they meet, and their experiences of how emotional events are managed and solved within their family, community, and the media. The first step in emotional literacy is being able to name, and therefore think about, emotions (Crow, 2005).

Children and young people at risk are those facing particular circumstances that place stress on them and their families. If we know these children and young people are at increased risk then it would be negligent of us not to pay attention to these young people by trying to address some of their emotional needs. This could be achieved by attempting to develop their self-worth, giving them the information they need, enabling a sense of achievement and providing some stability and safety.

Mental health promotion work focuses on the systems around children and families in particular circumstances by raising awareness of the issues and developing collaborative action around emotional needs. This means that individual children do not get pathologised and stigmatised, which can leave children and young people feeling that they are the problem rather than the situation being to blame.

The programmes are grounded in these theories of risk and resilience, self-esteem and emotional literacy. Each programme has activities that are specific to the client group but also has more general sessions that can be used with all groups of children and young people. Many of the Learning Mentors I have worked with have developed the ideas to use individually with the children they are supporting.

Each programme has its own introduction giving reasons why the particular group of young people were chosen and the process that informed the membership of the groups.

Promoting positive mental health is a key requirement and is implicit in many current policies such as *Every Child Matters: Change for Children* (2004) and the *National Service Framework for Children, Young People and Maternity Services* (2004). It is now well-recorded that positive mental health and educational achievement are intimately linked. The government has an emotional health and wellbeing strand in the Healthy School programme. This is very supportive of mental health promotion work and whole school approaches to emotional health and wellbeing for both staff and pupils. The Social and Emotional Aspects of Learning (SEAL) is an example of these developments in primary schools. The programme provides a range of resources for schools to look at key aspects of emotional health such as stress, changes and positive coping. The programme focuses on five major qualities and skills that underpin all aspects of life and help us to manage. These include: self-awareness, managing feelings, motivation, empathy and social skills. One aspect of the SEAL programme is to develop work with children and young people who are considered to be vulnerable. The resources provided throughout this book can be a useful addition to developing this work in your school environment. The Social Emotional and Behavioural Skills Programme is being developed for use in secondary schools.

How to use the Programmes

At the beginning of the programme you should provide each young person with a folder to store the work safely. These will contain activity sheets, any work they produce during the sessions and their evaluation forms. The sheets in each session should be printed from the CD-ROM included with this book.

When an activity belongs to one particular session you will find it printed as a thumbnail at the end of the session notes.

Each session includes notes for the facilitator, which explain the aims and how to run the activities.

The sessions are flexible and activities can be carried over to following sessions if discussion from the participants becomes important. The majority of sessions are managed comfortably within an hour if the session starts on time and the participants are engaged in the process. Every session ends with an evaluation sheet.

Evaluation sheets

The purpose of the evaluation sheet is to encourage the young people to have a voice in the process of the group. Facilitators should be flexible and be able to adapt the programme to take account of the evaluation provided by the individuals taking part in the group.

Explain to the young people that their honest assessment of the group is valuable and that without their comments and contributions the facilitators cannot find out what worked well and what did not. It can be difficult for some young people to be critical of the programme. This can be because of the strong relationships built up within the group.

The evaluation sheets in themselves serve as an activity, helping the young people to express their likes and dislikes and becoming more self-aware.

If the facilitator explains to the young person that the evaluation serves as an activity for them to understand themselves better, they are more likely to be honest in their assessment of the activities.

This publication provides you with four separate and complete programme of sessions to use with different groups. All the activity sheets are available to print from the CD-ROM. One copy of an evaluation sheet is included as a standard, appropriate for all the sessions, with a space in which to write the session number. See the sample overleaf.

Evaluation sheet example

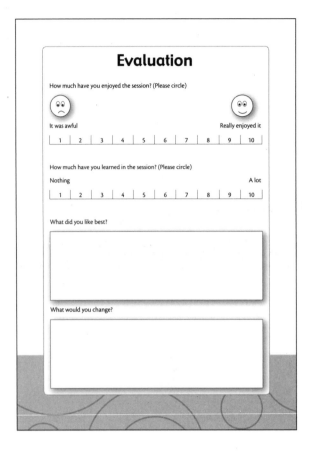

Copy the evaluation pages for each session; one copy so that the young people can have a record of their involvement and the other copy for the group records. Ask them to fill in the programme name and the session number.

Practitioners are frequently asked to provide evidence to justify their work. The evaluation serves to reinforce the benefits of running groupwork. It also helps in the planning of a programme, which can evolve to meet the needs of future groups.

Points to consider in running a group

▸ It is important that each young person is given a parental consent form before the beginning of the group so that parental permission is gained.

▸ Apart from the vulnerable children's activities, which were developed to work in an informal environment and with children and young people dipping in and out of the work, the other groupwork programmes have been developed for closed groups. Closed groups enable the establishment of a safe environment, with membership being decided at the beginning of the group and not changing.

▸ It may also be necessary to modify sessions according to the time available. The programmes are not set in stone and you can be flexible about some of the ice breakers and trust games. If the session or lesson is only 50 minutes long it may be hard to fit in all the activities. If the lesson lasts for over an hour it may be worth having a few more games to fall back on that fit with the activities for that session.

▸ The programmes have been written to work with groups of between three and 12 young people. If you are working with one or two young people then you can draw out some of the activities as a focus for your discussion. All the activities in the vulnerable children's programme can be used individually. Others include the Lifeline, Role models, Agony aunt and Stone therapy.

▸ The closed group programmes, working with just boys or girls and the course promoting mental health and wellbeing, are planned for pupils in secondary schools 11-16 years old. They can also be used with pupils in a primary school setting in Year 6 (10-11 year olds). The vulnerable children's programme can be adapted to a wide age range and was piloted successfully with children and young people ranging in age from 5 to 14.

▸ Consider the needs of all the participants. Ice breakers and trust games might need modifications for young people with a disability or sensory impairment.

▸ The issue of stability, safety and consistency are important factors in contributing to a successful group work programme. Using the same venue and room every week is recommended. This can be difficult to maintain in a busy secondary school.

▸ Many of the activities in the closed groups take place in rounds, sitting in a circle on chairs matched for height. The room should be suitable for this formation.

Certificates for each Programme:

This is to certify that

_____

has participated in and successfuly completed the

Resilience and Self-esteem
Group Work Programme

Signed _____ Date _____

This is to certify that

_____

has participated in and successfuly completed the

Just for Lads
Group Work Programme

Signed _____ Date _____

This is to certify that

_____

has participated in and successfuly completed the

Girls' Own
Group Work Programme

Signed _____ Date _____

This is to certify that

_____

has participated in and successfuly completed the

Healthy Minds
Group Work Programme

Signed _____ Date _____

Resources for Learning Mentors

Conclusion

Children need the resources to adapt successfully to changing physical, psychological and social environments. Where children are well-resourced within themselves, within their family and social contexts, a capacity to constructively adapt to adversity or resilience can be promoted. The activities contained within this programme give children an opportunity to begin building up their repertoire of coping in an empowering and supportive way.

There is an increased focus on preventative work that looks at resilience as a measure of young people's ability to deal with adversity. More preventative strategies should be developed to address the needs of vulnerable groups. Homeless children and young people certainly fall into this category and it is hoped that the activities contained within this programme will give others confidence to work with these young people in an empowering way and become a listening ear and support for the young people and their families.

Working in community bases already routinely accessed by vulnerable families seems a logical way to avoid stigmatising and pathologising these young people. This is not to say that the stress and adversity that they may have encountered should not be recognised, but by listening to and validating these experiences these young people will be able to move towards making sense of their experiences.

Developing preventative work also reduces structural barriers historically inherent in Child and Adolescent Mental Health Services; such initiatives reduce discrimination and inequality and promote access and inclusion.

References

Adams, J. (1997) *Girlpower – How Far Does It Go?* A Resource and Training Pack on Young Women and Self-Esteem, Published by Sheffield Centre for HIV and Sexual Health.

Allen, P., Warwick, I. & Begum, J. (2004) *New in our Nation, Activities to promote self esteem and resilience in young asylum seekers*. Bristol: Lucky Duck Publishing

Allen, P., Harper, B. & Rowell, J. (2004) *You are Welcome, Activities to promote self-esteem and resilience in children from diverse communities, including asylum seekers and refugees*. Bristol: Lucky Duck Publishing.

Borba, M. (2001) *The Five Building Blocks of Self-esteem*. Available at: http://www.micheleborba.com/Pages/5buildingBlocks.htm [accessed 29.7.2006]

Crow, G. & Allen, P. (2005) *Promoting Mental Health and Emotional Wellbeing*. Unpublished.

Curry, M. & Bromfield, C. (1995) *Education for Primary Schools Through Circle Time*. NASEN Publications.

Daniel, B., Wassel, S. & Gilligan, R. (1999) *Child Development for Child Care and Protection Workers*. London: Jessica Kingsley Publishers.

Department of Health (2005) *Mental Health of Children and Young People in Great Britain 2004*.

Department for Skills and Education (2001) *Promoting Children's Mental Health within Early Years and School Settings*. DfEE Publications.

Fonagy P., Steele M., Steele H., Higgit, A. & Target, M. (1994). *Theory and practice of resilience*. Journal of Child Psychology and Psychiatry, 35, 231-257.

Fuller, A. (2001) *Background Paper on Resilience* (presented to the Northern Territory Principals Association)

Gilligan, C. (1990). *Joining the Resistance: Psychology, politics, girls and women*. Michigan Quarterly Review, 24(4), 501-536.

Gilligan, R. (1997). *Beyond permanence? The importance of resilience in child placement practice and planning*. Adoption and Fostering, 21 (1), 12-20.

Goleman, D. (1995) *Emotional Intelligence*. New York: Bantam cited in Maines, B. (2003) *Reading Faces and learning about Human Emotions*. Bristol: Lucky Duck.

Gross, R.D. (1995) *Psychology: the Science of Mind and Behaviour*. London: Hodder and Stoughton Publishers.

Harvey, M. (1999) *Mind Matters: A resource bank on relationships: "Work it out"*. U.K Youth Publications

Harvey, M. (2000) *Mind Matters: A resource bank on self-esteem: "What if...?"* U.K Youth Publications

Health Education Authority (1999) *World Mental Health Day Activity Sheets*.

Lloyd, T. (1997) *'Let's get Changed Lads', Developing work with boys and young men*. Published by Working with Men.

Marcotte, D., Alain, M., & Gosselin, M.-J. (1999). *Gender differences in adolescent depression: Gender-typed characteristics or problem-solving skills deficits?* Sex Roles: A Journal of Research, 41(1), 31-48.

Page, A., Ainsworth, A. & Pett, M. (1993) *Homeless families and their children's health problems: a Utah urban experience*. Western Journal of Medicine, 158, 30-35.

Powell, T. (1992) *Progressive Muscle Relaxation*.

Peace Foundation Sheffield *Stilling*.

Smithers, R. (2006) *'This has made me feel normal'*. Guardian Education Supplement. May 16th. p.3

Vostanis, P., Grattan, E., Cumella, S., et al (1997) *Psychosocial functioning of homeless children*. Journal of the American Academy of Child and Adolescent Psychiatry, 36, 881-889

Vostanis, P. (2002) *Mental Health of Homeless children and their families*. Advances in Psychiatric Treatment, 8: 463 - 469.

Webb, E., Shankleman, J., Evans, M., et al (2001) *The health of children in refuges for women victims of domestic violence*. BMJ, 323, 210-213.

Working With Men, (1999) *Male Image Photo pack*.

White, M. (1999) *Magic Circles: Building Self-esteem through Circle Time*. Bristol: Lucky Duck Publishing

www.childstress.com

www.mind.org.uk

www.academy.umd.edu/scholarship/featured_research.htm (Tracey T Manning, 2002)

Programme 1

Activities to promote self-esteem, emotional literacy and resilience in vulnerable children and young people

Developed in collaboration with the Interim Accommodation Staff in Sheffield

Contents

On the CD-ROM

○ Evaluation Sheet

○ About Me

○ My Window

○ I Am Cool Because

○ Cool News Inc.

○ If I Had a Magic Wand

○ Important People

○ My Best Friend Is...

○ My Best Friend Thinks...

○ My Group

○ Everyone Is Different

○ 11 x Emotions

○ Body

○ Physical Symptoms of Stress

○ Signs of Stress

○ Physical, Emotional and Behavioural Signs of Stress

○ What Causes Stress?

○ Tips To Beat Stress

○ Sid The Snail Storyboard

○ Maisy Loses Her Home Storyboard

○ The Day I Lost My Home

○ 2 x Word Association Cards

○ 7 x Poems

○ This Is My Shield

○ Certificate

Foreword

Vulnerable groups of children and young people, such as those who are homeless, have diverse needs which are usually not met by existing services. Limited interventions usually respond to crises and severe problems rather than enhance young people's resilience. Reasons include the overall lack of preventive services, the complexity and mobility of this young client group, the non-engaging or inaccessible nature of services and therapeutic interventions, and the fragmentation between the voluntary and the non-statutory sector.

This refreshing package of therapeutic activities in collaboration with the Interim Accommodation Site staff is a reflection of addressing a number of these issues. The package for group therapeutic activities is engaging and friendly, accommodating a range of developmental and communication needs, and combining practical support, fun, social interaction and components of therapeutic frameworks (interpersonal, cognitive, problem-solving, exploration of feelings). These are applied at a preventive (universal rather than targeted) level for all young people facing similar adverse circumstances, with the aim of building up their coping strategies, self-efficacy and self-esteem.

The package is underpinned by the authors' experience and the partnership between different agencies working with homeless young people. The pack is nicely complemented by well thought through, user-friendly, and easy to administer and analyse evaluation worksheets. This evidence-base approach will be valuable in its future use across different services.

The pack of therapeutic activities has also been successfully applied with young refugee and asylum-seeking young people, and could easily be adapted for similar vulnerable groups such as young offenders or young people looked after by local authorities.

Panos Vostanis

Professor of Child and Adolescent Psychiatry

University of Leicester

Introduction

The pilot of the vulnerable children's work was initiated by the work on promoting resilience and self-esteem in asylum seeker children and young people. The Homeless Assessment and Support Team (HAST) had seen reports on the development of the groupwork programmes to support these vulnerable young people and had approached Child and Adolescent Primary Mental Health Services to consider whether such a resource could be adapted to meet some of the needs presented by young homeless school aged children living in interim accommodation in Sheffield. The focus of the work was to be delivered in the interim accommodation play resource centres, which are attached to the interim accommodation sites. As my remit was to service the North of Sheffield it was agreed to pilot the work in this locality. Fortunately the Homeless Children's Development Worker was keen to engage with this work and the pilot got underway in November 2004.

Homeless families are defined as all adults with dependant children who are statutorily accepted by local authorities (housing departments) in the UK, and are usually accommodated for a brief period in voluntary, local authority or housing association hostels. This period varies from a few days to several months. The pilot was delivered in the local authority interim accommodation site in the North of Sheffield.

The reason for family homelessness is largely due to domestic violence and to a lesser extent harassment from neighbours (Vostanis et al. 1997).

Homeless children and their parents have a range of health needs; children are more likely to have low birth weight, anaemia, dental decay and delayed immunisations, to be of lower stature and have a greater degree of nutritional stress. They are also more likely to suffer accidents, injuries and burns. A substantial number of homeless children have delayed development compared with the general population. This includes specific developmental delays, such as in receptive and expressive language and visual, motor and reading skills, as well as general skills and educational status (Page et al. 1993; Webb et al. 2001; Vostanis, 2002).

The social profile of homeless children makes them vulnerable to a number of risk factors increasing the likelihood of developing mental health problems and disorders.

The mobility of homeless children and families makes it difficult for them to access mainstream services from either health or local authorities. Developing preventative approaches and building the capacity of frontline workers to deal and work effectively with the emotional needs of such children should therefore be a priority for primary child and adolescent mental health services.

The interim accommodation staff had identified some common needs that the children and young people had:

▸ emotional immaturity, such as the inability to show a range of emotions in an appropriate manner

▸ issues around lack of confidence and low self-esteem

▸ lack of attachment in relationships and no long-term friendships.

▸ issues around the development of social skills within the family and community

▸ potential and real signs of developing mental health problems.

The programme aim was to provide some useful resources and practical activities to promote the emotional wellbeing and resilience of children and young people in temporary accommodation. The session activities had to be developed so that children and young people could access them in an informal play environment. They also had to be developed so that children and young people could participate in as many of the activities as they chose. Each activity needed to be able to stand alone so that children and young people could benefit from taking part in one or all of the activities. This was taking account of the transient nature of the population of children and young people and the fact that it was impossible to determine numbers and length of time they may be accessing homeless services to enable the establishment of a closed group

Many obstacles were anticipated:

- ‣ low attention span and 'special needs'
- ‣ language barriers
- ‣ large age range (formally 5 -14 but in reality 0 -19 including parents)
- ‣ differing abilities and interests
- ‣ families staying on site from between a week and a year
- ‣ children and young people arrive on site at different times from school
- ‣ that the playroom had open access (children came and went as they pleased)
- ‣ other activities going on a the same time (pool, outdoor games, arts and crafts)
- ‣ parents coming and going and staff having to deal with other issues that they need to raise
- ‣ the atmosphere on the site, for example families falling out with each other, tensions caused by racism and so on.

It was hoped that as a result of this work the children and young people would gain a greater ability to cope with various aspects of their lives both now and in the future, that the children would feel more able to understand and show their emotions and respond appropriately, and that their confidence and self-esteem would be raised through fun, games, discussion and reassurance.

To give a snapshot of the children living on the interim accommodation site, during the autumn term 2004, 36 children and young people aged 4 to 16 years moved onto the site. Of this group, 23 were white British and three were white British and Caribbean, ten were from the Middle East, Europe, Africa, and Asia and did not speak English as a first language; six of whom were refugees and four were 'habitual residents' from Portugal.

The group of 36 attended a total of 22 different schools between them, of which 15 were primary schools and seven were secondary schools. Of these young people, five were not on a school role when they arrived, 11 changed schools on arrival and 15 had or expected to change schools when they moved off site. A further 24 of the children had attended more than the standard one or two schools (depending on whether they were primary or secondary) and had changed schools between one and five times.

Out of these young people, ten had formerly identified Special Education Needs and another five had received a total of 16 days in fixed term exclusions. 19 had to get the bus because their school was not local and six others went by car for the same reason. Ten walked to a local school each day.

In July 2005, 31 children and young people had moved off the site with their families, but five were still there and had spent between 48 and 60 weeks in this temporary situation. Of the 31 that had moved, they had spent an average of 29 weeks on site before moving.

The play workers felt that they were already promoting the emotional wellbeing of children and young people in their work. However, having dedicated space and time to focus on a project that was specifically designed to address these issues meant that all the workers could identify the meaning and purpose of the activities, thus enabling them to understand the benefits to children and young people with a clear focus. It was felt that the work equipped them to think about why the activities were being used rather than just focussing on the activity itself.

Being open and honest facilitated the pilot of this work, and helped develop good working relationships. This meant that we could adapt and change ideas in a supportive and positive way to the benefit of the young people taking part in the project.

One key consideration when undertaking this work is to be aware of conflicting priorities. The play workers needed to consider holiday periods when much of their work is focused on themes for these times, such as Christmas, Easter and holiday play schemes. Workers also needed to be aware of their own and environmental limitations and choose activities that they felt comfortable and confident using.

Some of the comments about the different activities that the children and young people found useful included: 'Writing what I like and don't like,' 'They make you think about how you are,' 'When I had my emotions photo took,' 'Painting and the short video,' and, 'I was proud doing it'.

Comments from the play workers included: 'An excellent session which felt very valuable, it made the kids think and fed their imaginations.' The workers were sometimes surprised by the level of involvement that some young people displayed. Comments included: 'They had engaged and enjoyed the activities without too much encouragement,' 'I was really impressed with the comments that the other kids made about each other,' 'The kids seemed really relaxed and the sessions were a lot calmer.' The sessions have inspired the play workers to further develop the work and to develop 'activities with a purpose'. Activities that they would like to develop included, emotional literacy, racial awareness, teamwork, bullying, being different, grief and loss, puberty, drugs awareness, self-worth, participation and healthy eating.

Although the programme was designed and piloted specifically with children and young people living in interim accommodation in mind, the activities and preventative nature of the programme means that it can be used and adapted to a variety of settings and vulnerable groups.

The programme

There were various processes that necessarily preceded the pilot work of the programme. Meetings took place to help the workers define what support they wanted and how this could be translated into work on the ground. Time was spent at the play session to get a feel of the organisation and running of the service. It was agreed that we would produce resources and pilot them, asking the play workers for their views and evaluation of how well they felt the children and young people had received them. We also asked the children and young people themselves what they thought about the activities and what they would change. In this way the process of engagement, capacity building, learning and sharing was achieved.

The play workers took an active role in commenting on the resources and ideas that we had developed and gave opinions about what they felt would work. They also made suggestions about what materials would work better for some of the activities.

Working collaboratively with others is key to our work. It develops multi-agency links, builds capacity, enriches the work, shares the workload, and helps embed the ideas and activities into service delivery, supporting the continuation and sustainability of the work.

This programme aims to provide some useful resources and practical activities to promote the emotional wellbeing and resilience of vulnerable children and young people. The session activities have been developed so that children and young people can access them in an informal play environment. They have also been developed so that children and young people can participate in as many of the activities as they choose to. Each activity can stand-alone so that children and young people can benefit from taking part in one or all of the activities. This is taking account of the transient nature of some populations of vulnerable children and young people and the fact that it is impossible to determine numbers and length of time they may be accessing different services to enable the establishment of a closed group.

The programme is based on the premise that by listening to and learning from others, children and young people develop a greater sense of themselves.

Emotional literacy

Emotional literacy is the ability to recognise, understand and articulate feelings in relation to oneself and other people, and the capacity to develop constructive coping strategies to manage life's stresses. It is increasingly acknowledged that emotional literacy contributes to emotional wellbeing and can be promoted in a variety of health, social services and education settings. If a child is given insufficient emotional nurturance this can lead to poor mental health in both childhood and adulthood.

Children and young people who are resilient have a number of protective factors. Such factors reside in the qualities of the young person, their families and their communities. Interpersonal and intra-personal protective factors such as self-esteem, sociability, autonomy, positive coping strategies, a positive attitude, a problem-solving approach, good communication skills and a capacity to reflect are all related to psychological resilience. Developing resilience does not mean that young people will become immune to stress but that they will be more likely to recover from negative events. Daniel et al (1999) identified three fundamental building blocks that underpin resilience:

1. a secure base, somewhere that the young person feels secure and belongs

2. good self-esteem, feeling competent and having an internal sense of worth

3. a sense of self-efficacy, having an understanding of personal strengths and weaknesses and a sense of mastery and control.

Protective factors within the family are a reflection of patterns of family interaction that are warm, cohesive and supportive. Community protective factors are a reflection of the support and influence of peers and a feeling of support from an adult outside of the family.

It is hoped that this programme will allow children to:

▸ raise self-esteem

▸ improve listening skills

▸ increase insight and awareness

▸ build confidence

▸ enhance friendships

▸ develop individual coping strategies

▸ facilitate working together co-operatively

▸ offer understanding

▸ explore feelings

▸ have fun!

How to use the programme

At the beginning of the programme provide each young person with a folder to store the work safely. These will contain any work they produce during the sessions and their evaluation forms. The sheets for each session should be printed from the CD-ROM that accompanies this book.

The sessions are organised as follows:

▸ Session 1 focuses on the participants, their likes and dislikes, and involves activity sheets that can be used over a number of sessions.

▸ Session 2 focuses on emotional literacy which helps children to label and state emotions in a creative way and can also take a number of sessions to complete.

- Session 3 looks at how are bodies and minds can be affected by positive rewards and also negative stress.

- Session 4 focuses on different mediums that children and young people can use to express feelings, learn coping strategies and their own personal strengths

When an activity sheet belongs to one particular session you will find it printed at the end of the session notes.

Each session includes notes for the facilitator. These explain the aims and how to run the activities. At the end of each session there is an evaluation sheet.

Evaluation sheets

The purpose of the evaluation sheet is for the children to have a voice in the process. We believe that facilitators should be flexible and be able to adapt the programme to reflect the evaluation by the individuals taking part in the sessions. You should clearly state to the children that you value their honest assessment of the activities and, without their comments and contributions, you cannot know what works and what doesn't. It is helpful to get the children to complete the forms with the support of a facilitator. This helps children understand what they are being asked for, especially if literacy skills are an issue.

The evaluation serves to reinforce the benefits of being allowed to run such programmes in a variety of settings. Practitioners are increasingly being asked to provide evidence to justify their work. The evaluation serves to reinforce arguments for being allowed to run preventative programmes. It also helps inform changes to the programme so that it evolves to meet the needs of future participants.

Session One

Introducing Me

Aims

▸ To provide a variety of activity sheets that enable children and young people to become aware of their likes and dislikes.

▸ To promote awareness of factors that influence the way we feel about ourselves.

▸ For participants to understand that everyone has strengths, weaknesses, similarities and differences.

Plan for the session

1. 'About Me' activity sheet

2. 'My Window' activity sheet

3. 'I am Cool Because...' activity sheet

4. 'Cool News Inc.' activity sheet

5. 'If I Had A Magic Wand' activity sheet

6. 'Important People' activity sheet

7. 'My Best Friend' activity sheet

8. 'My Best Friend Thinks...' activity sheet

9. 'My Group' activity sheet

10. 'Everyone is Different' activity sheet.

Materials

▸ Folder

▸ Activity sheets

▸ Pens and pencils

▸ Coloured pencils or pens

▸ Polaroid camera and film

▸ Glue

▸ Evaluation sheets.

Introducing me

Session One includes a variety of activity sheets that have been produced to help participants to think about their positive qualities and their likes and dislikes. It is important that the activity sheets are given to the participants in the order that they appear in the pack so that they begin by looking at general concepts about themselves and build on this awareness throughout the course of the work.

Lay out the materials needed for the participants to complete the activity sheets. Encourage participation but ensure that other children and young people who do not want to take part do not spoil or comment on the work being produced by those participating.

Give each participant a plain, light coloured folder to keep their work in. Encourage the participants to decorate and personalise their folders.

You may need to assist some participants with filling in the writing element on the activity sheets.

Give the participants the 'About Me' activity sheet to complete.

With prior permission from the participants take a polaroid or digital photograph of each participant.

Once developed or printed the participants can glue their photograph onto the 'About Me' sheet.

Encourage the participants to complete other activity sheets about themselves: 'My Window', 'I Am Cool Because...', and 'Cool News Inc.'. The participants can choose to fill in all the activity sheets or a selection from those mentioned. End this session with 'If I Had A Magic Wand'.

Once this session has been completed the participants can move on to thinking about wider issues that affect them. Begin with asking the participants to think about those people in their lives that are important to them and encourage the participants to complete the activity sheet 'Important People'.

In the next part ask the participants to think about what other people are like.

Encourage the participants to complete the activity sheets, 'My Best Friend Is...', 'My Best Friend Thinks' and 'My Group'.

End by encouraging the participants to complete the 'Everyone Is Different' activity sheet. This last activity sheet helps the participants to consider qualities outside of themselves and to begin to develop awareness about difference and diversity.

Activity Sheets for Session One:

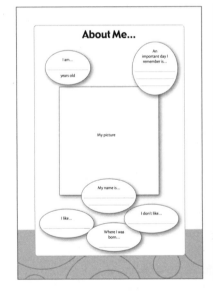

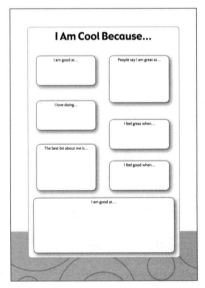

Activity Sheets for Session One continued:

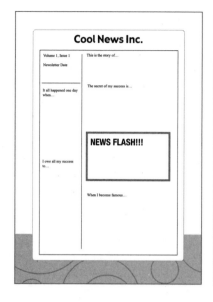

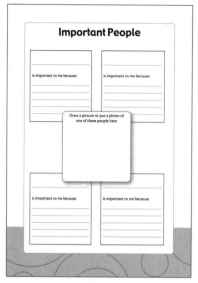

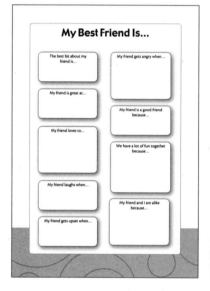

Session Two

Facing Feelings

Aims

- ▸ to introduce and learn about emotions and feelings
- ▸ to help children to express feelings in a safe way
- ▸ to enable children to label feelings
- ▸ to explore the relationship between emotions and facial expressions
- ▸ to begin to explore the different kinds of life events that can provoke strong feelings in us.

Plan for the session

1. Expressing Feelings
2. Clay Faces.

Materials

- ▸ 'Emotions' activity sheets
- ▸ Clay
- ▸ Modelling tools
- ▸ Paints
- ▸ Velcro sticky patches
- ▸ Pens
- ▸ Card
- ▸ Video camera
- ▸ Evaluation sheets.

Expressing feelings

This activity is designed to help children and young people identify facial expressions that are associated with certain emotions.

Lay out the materials needed for the participants to complete the worksheets. Encourage participation but ensure that other children and young people who do not want to take part do not spoil or comment on the work being produced by those participating.

You may need to assist some participants with filling in the writing element on the activity sheets.

Give the participants the 'Emotions' activity sheets to complete. Encourage the participants to complete the activity sheets and support the participants to discuss their thoughts about the emotions being expressed. This activity will enable participants to think about an emotion they would like to express for the next activity.

This sample activity sheet is one of a set for you to print in colour from the CD-ROM. The other emotions represented are:

Sad	Angry	xcited	Disgusted	Kind
Hurt	Surprised	Afraid	Sorry	Interested

The facilitator can make a selection appropriate for the group members.

Clay Faces

Clay Faces is a creative activity that allows children to explore their feelings around issues they choose and to create a clay face that reflects that feeling.

Place the materials on the table and encourage children and young people to participate. Explain that participants can make a face that reflects an emotion they have had over something that has happened in their life. You can use the images from the previous activity to help participants choose an emotion.

Examples can include:

Sad that you lost something

Angry when you got told off at school or home

Upset when someone called you a name

Frightened when someone dared you to do something you really didn't want to do

Happy when you got a present that you really wanted

Excited when you went onto a big roller-coaster

Frustrated when you found it difficult to do something

Worried when you got lost somewhere.

The participants make an egg shape with the clay, which is then cut in half so that the back of the 'face' is flat. On the oval side the participants make the face show the emotion they want to portray. It is worthwhile for the workers to make their own face alongside the participants so that they can demonstrate an emotion and their interpretation of that emotion onto the face and explain to the participants what caused them to feel that emotion.

Once the face has been made encourage the participants to write the emotion underneath the face and say what caused them to feel that emotion. Expressing feelings through the clay faces provides a safe way for children to express feelings, which they may otherwise be unable to do if asked directly.

The face is then left to dry for the following week.

Once the clay is dry encourage the participants to film their clay faces with them expressing their emotion and saying out loud the reason they felt that way.

Activity Sheets for Section 2:

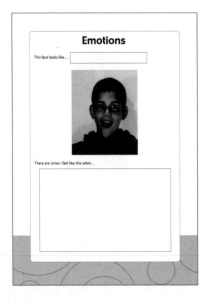

1 of 11 activity sheets

Session Three

Body Work

Aims

▸ To encourage children and young people to accept positive feedback.

▸ To introduce the concept that are bodies are affected by our emotions.

▸ To examine what causes us stress and to recognise the general components of stress.

Plan for session

1. My Body

2. Mind and Body

3. Stress

Materials

▸ Large roll of paper or wallpaper or light coloured fabric, cotton/muslin.

▸ Pens, glitter pens, marker pens, fabric pens

▸ Sequins, glue, felt, butterfly clips

▸ Coloured paper, card

▸ Pencil crayons

▸ Paint

▸ Template of body shape

▸ Digital camera

▸ Body template

▸ Evaluation sheets.

My body

This activity is designed to encourage children and young people to be able to give and receive positive feedback in a fun and creative way.

Encourage participants to draw around each other's bodies on the fabric or paper provided.

Once they have drawn around each other ask the other participants in the session to write or say one or more positive comments about each participant.

Be aware of participants who are struggling with writing skills and support them or encourage other children and young people to support them if necessary.

Ensure that only positive comments are written about each participant.

Once all comments from this session have been added the participants can decorate their bodies with the materials provided.

The participants' 'bodies' can be stored safely for use in future sessions if required. Participants can add to the positive comments as they get to know each other better. Workers can also bring out the participants' 'body' in future sessions when they have noticed a child doing something positive.

If space is an issue then a body shape on A2 paper without the head can be used. The participants are encouraged to decorate their bodies. Digital photographs can be taken of the participants expressing emotions, such as sadness, happiness, anger, frustration, worry, surprise and so on. The photographs can then be printed onto A4 paper and attached to the body with butterfly clips. The participants can display the face representing the mood they want to. Comments from the other participants can be added to these bodies in the same way as they would have been added to the large bodies.

Alternatively you can just use the emotions images and encourage participants to make a collage of their photographs with the comments added.

Mind and body

This activity is designed to encourage participants to begin to think about the connection between our thoughts, feelings and behaviour.

Once the participants have completed decorating their bodies encourage them to think about how their body would feel when they are:

Excited

Sad

Frightened

Lonely

Angry

Stressed.

If you use one of the photographs of the participant expressing an emotion ask her to explain how her body might feel if she was experiencing this emotion. If not use the examples of emotions from Session Two. Ask the participants what behaviour might be the result of someone feeling this way.

Give out the template of the body and ask participants to write the feelings they have stated onto the body where they may experience that sensation.

Once they have done this ask the participants to write down the kinds of behaviours that they might expect if someone was feeling this way.

This will help the participants to understand the connection between our emotions, thoughts and feelings; the physical reactions in our bodies to our emotions and the consequences of such emotions on our behaviour and actions.

Stress

This activity is designed to help participants understand the nature of stress and to think about healthy ways of dealing with stress and pressure in our lives.

Give out the 'Signs of Stress' activity sheet and ask the participants to fill it in. It is important that facilitators explain to the participants that recognising the signs of stress is one of the first steps in helping them develop healthy coping to deal with stress. Give out the 'Physical Symptoms of Stress' activity sheet and the 'Physical, Emotional and Behavioural Signs of Stress' activity sheet. Discuss with the participants any symptoms that they did not think was a sign of stress.

What is stress?

Distribute the 'What Causes Us Stress?' activity sheet and encourage participants to think about the things that cause them stress in their lives and all the things they do that helps to relieve these feelings of stress.

Explain that stress is a natural reaction to lots and lots of demands and pressure. It is not an illness. But if there is a lot of stress or if it goes on for a long time it can lead to health problems.

Stress is the way our bodies react to change.

These feelings can come from situations or people and can be good or bad.

Most people see stress as worry, tension and pressure but not all stress is bad. We need stress in our lives or life would be dull.

They way we think and feel about a situation can make stress good or bad. For example, if you are moving house and were happy and excited about this, this would be a good stress, but if you were anxious and scared about moving then this would have a negative impact.

The demands placed on you have to be greater than your resources to cope with these demands for stress to have a negative impact.

Why do we get stressed?

Flight and fight

Our reaction to stress is a primitive response. Humans developed instinctive reactions to dangerous situations in order to survive.

At the sight of danger or perceived threat our hypothalamus sends a message to our adrenal glands and within seconds we can run faster, jump higher, hit harder and hear and see better.

In modern society there are no longer wild animals that threaten us buts lots of competing and complex demands on our time, emphasis on the way we look and queries about doing the right thing, which can all trigger the same bodily reactions.

If the participants are struggling with thinking of ways that they deal with stress then help them with suggesting some healthy coping, Ask them what they like to do to relax or have fun. Alternatively hand out the sheet 'Tips to Beat Stress'. Discuss with the participants if there are any items on the list that they already do or any that they think they would consider trying.

Activity Sheets for Session Three:

Body

Signs of Stress

Look at the list of symptoms. Decide which ones are caused by stress. Put an arrow from the symptom to the body part for all these symptoms that you think can be related to stress.

Nervous
Itchy skin/rashes
Relaxed
Perspiration/sweat
Forgetfulness
Carelessness
Nightmares
Find it hard to sleep
Burping
Go off your food
Butterflies in your stomach
Stomach-aches
Going to the toilet more
Headaches
Sneezing
Cold
Angry outbursts
Laughing
Lose your sense of humour

Anxious/fretting
Excited
Fast heartbeat
Lack of concentration
Boredom
Diarrhoea
Ear ache
Cramps
Overeat
Feel sick
Can't make your mind up
Flatulence/break wind a lot
Feeling sad/depressed
Feel tired all the time/lethargy
Runny nose
Feeling irritable/tetchy/moody
Smiling
Getting grumpy all the time

Physical, Emotional and Behavioural Signs of Stress

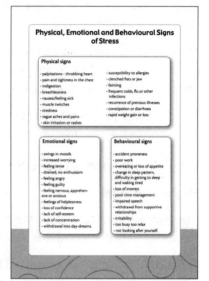

Physical signs

- palpitations - throbbing heart
- pain and tightness in the chest
- indigestion
- breathlessness
- nausea/feeling sick
- muscle twitches
- tiredness
- vague aches and pains
- skin irritation or rashes
- susceptibility to allergies
- clenched fists or jaw
- fainting
- frequent colds, flu or other infections
- recurrence of previous illnesses
- constipation or diarrhoea
- rapid weight gain or loss

Emotional signs

- swings in moods
- increased worrying
- feeling tense
- drained, no enthusiasm
- feeling angry
- feeling guilty
- feeling nervous, apprehensive or anxious
- feelings of helplessness
- loss of confidence
- lack of self-esteem
- lack of concentration
- withdrawal into day-dreams.

Behavioural signs

- accident proneness
- poor work
- overeating or loss of appetite
- change in sleep pattern, difficulty in getting to sleep and waking tired
- loss of interest
- poor time management
- impaired speech
- withdrawal from supportive relationships
- irritability
- too busy too relax
- not looking after yourself.

Physical Symptoms of Stress

Muscles tense up, ready for action. Your neck and shoulder muscles can feel tense and sore and can make your neck and back ache.

Your brain sends a message, which gets more adrenaline in your body. This can make you headachy or dizzy. Your mind becomes alert or can become confused.

Blood-clotting ability increases preparing for possible injury.

Your pupils widen. This can make your eyesight feel wobbly.

Nostrils and air passages in lungs open wider to get more air in quickly.

Heart beat speeds up. Blood pressure rises. Blood goes faster around your body. Sweating increases to help cool the body. Your blood comes up near the surface of the skin. This means you can go red/blush more and sweat more.

Blood is diverted to the muscles and you can look 'pale with fright'.

Immune responses decrease. Helpful in the short term to allow massive response to immediate threat. Harmful over a long period.

Liver releases sugar to provide quick energy. This can make your tummy feel unsettled and wobbly. Your tummy also slows down because the blood goes to other parts to help them when you are worried.

The muscles around your bowels and bladder (sphincter muscles) relax, making you want to go to the toilet more often. They also contract to close openings of bowels and bladder.

What Causes Us Stress?

Write in all the things that you can think of that cause you stress.

Write in all the things that you can think of that help to combat stress.

Tips to Beat Stress
(from: www.childstress.com)

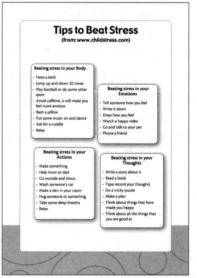

Beating stress in your Body

- Have a bath
- Jump up and down 20 times
- Play football or do some other sport
- Avoid caffeine, it will make you feel more anxious
- Bash a pillow
- Put some music on and dance
- Ask for a cuddle
- Relax

Beating stress in your Emotions

- Tell someone how you feel
- Write it down
- Draw how you feel
- Watch a happy video
- Go and talk to your pet
- Phone a friend

Beating stress in your Actions

- Make something
- Help mum or dad
- Go outside and shout
- Wash someone's car
- Make a den in your room
- Hug someone or something
- Take some deep breaths
- Relax

Beating stress in your Thoughts

- Write a story about it
- Read a book
- Tape record your thoughts
- Do a tricky puzzle
- Make a plan
- Think about things that have made you happy
- Think about all the things that you are good at

Session Four

Coping and Strength

Aims

▶ To help children explore systems of support available to them

▶ To promote empathy and social skills

▶ To use a safe activity for children and young people to express their feelings

▶ To explore alternative media to express our feelings and thoughts

▶ To use story telling, drawing, poetry, rap or prose to discover ways to express personal stories.

▶ To help children build up a picture of their individual coping strategies and identity.

▶ To build up a personal profile in visual collage form of all the things that they find helpful and protective in their lives.

Plan for the sessions

1. Storyboards

2. Poetry

3. My Shield of Strength

4. Treasure Box

Materials

▶ 'Sid the Snail Storyboard' or 'Maisy Loses Her Home Storyboard' activity sheets

▶ 'Sid Loses His Shell' and 'The Day I Lost My Home' activity sheets

▶ Poetry

▶ Poetry paper

▶ Shield shapes on large card

▶ Travel brochures, catalogues, magazines

▶ Leaves, feathers, twigs, felt material, wood shavings

▶ Sequins, string, glitter pens, glue, sellotape

▶ Coloured paper, card, marker pens, pencil crayons, paint

▶ Clay

▶ Cardboard jewellery boxes

▶ Evaluation sheets.

Storyboards

The storyboard activity is intended to help participants think and express emotions about loss and change in a safe way. By using a story the participants can think about the impact on the character and consider what their own thoughts and feelings would be in the particular situation.

Give out the storyboard worksheets to the participants. Sid the Snail worksheets are intended for the younger participants and the Maisy Loses her Home is intended for the older participants. Encourage the participants to think about the characters in the stories and write what they would think and feel if they where in a similar situation. Participants can write about their thoughts and feelings of loss and upset in a safe way by using third person techniques to explore their own personal stories and feelings.

Once they have completed the storyboard participants can be encouraged to write their own story and draw their own images of Sid losing his shell or a young person losing his home.

Poetry

This activity is a creative session that encourages participants to think about their own life experiences and develop a poem that reflects those experiences. Writing down your emotions and feelings about issues is a therapeutic method of helping participants to make sense of the world and their experiences. Give out examples of poetry that have been written about what people think about their home, family, homelessness, change or any other topic that you feel is pertinent to the group you are working with. Encourage participants to read the poetry, be aware if participants are struggling with reading skills and read out the poetry for them. Hand out the poetry paper and encourage participants to write a poem, piece of prose or rap which reflects their own experiences. If children and young people are worried about their spelling ensure that you support and reassure them. Explain that the activity is not about their spelling skills but about being able to express their feelings. Hand out the word association cards to help participants think about words or ideas that they can use for their own work.

Ideas that participants came up with in the pilot of this programme included:

Design	School
Neighbours and friends	My bedroom
My house and family	The day I moved
My future	Caring for family
Ideal home	Making new friends
My hopes for the future	My pet I left behind
Looking after brothers and sisters	Fun we have in the playroom

My Home
In the winter there's snow and ice
In my home it's warm and nice
In my home I feel happy
Even when my mum is snappy
My brother Kurt's a funny fella
He plays outside in any weather
My mum is loving
My mum is kind
She keeps me safe all the time
Jamie

Playroom

I come to the cabin everyday
To see Matt, Saj and Sarah just to say
We laugh, we eat, we play and chat
Except for Matt, because he has his own way.
Then there's Saj
With his big nose,
He's not an expert when it comes to chores
The only talented thing about him
He's good at dogs when he's on all fours.
You can't forget about Sarah Dwand
She always has a smile on her face
You can count on her to give you a hand
But her coffee making... Oh what a disgrace!
But at the end of the day, they're all so nice
I don't know what to say.
Written by Kurtis

Homeless

Walking down the street
Thinking I am alone.
Yet there are millions of us
Without a real home.
Lonely and cold
Is how I spend my days.
I hate to think of those people
Who dash around in their disrespectful ways.
Hungry and in fear
I sit wishing people were here.
As much as I wish
My dreams still do not appear
But still I wish I had a home near.
Maria

Hopeless

Hopeless is how I feel, I can't do anything right.
On my own with no one to love,
My parents, how could they. They don't care about me.
Everyone stares at me and I feel dirty
Lonely in the midnight darkness, only a ripped coat covering me.
Empty, no one comes near the bins where I live.
Sad, sometimes I cry myself to sleep
Sorry for myself. I think why me?
Megan

Need

All alone
I sit at home
I wonder what you think when I stay home.
You probably think of a cosy warm fire and a cosy bed
But let me tell you something
My home has a fire, yes.
But the street is where I sleep.
My bed is cold
My life is empty
All I have and really need are my parents
They help to see me through.

Ashleigh

Shelter

Having no home is horrible
No solid ground to hold me
Not seeing my mum and dad
Makes the days long and lonely
For shelter I would be glad
Greedy people make me angry
With their perfect shoes and clothes
Wasting food and money
While my hunger grows
For shelter I would be glad

Amiee

Fear

I am all alone
I have no home
I don't want presents
I just want loving parents.
I feel scared
I get nightmares
With no support I am in fear
I just wish my home was near.
I always ask why
And then I just cry
A mum and a dad is something I've never had
I own nothing without that.
But how long will I last alone
Without a home
The end is near
Is what I fear!

Becky

(Permissions given by young people for reproduction of poems.)

My Shield of Strength

My Shield of Strength is a creative activity that looks at the things that make us feel strong and safe.

Workers organise the activity by displaying the materials on tables and encouraging the children to take part by explaining to the children that they can build and decorate a shield that is personal to them.

Give out the shield shapes. You can either cut them out on large pieces of card or blow up the template onto A3 size paper. Hand out the magazines and ask the children to fill in the sections on the shield. They can use the sections as a guide to think about their own coping skills, their main supports and their wish for the future.

The workers ask the children to think about all the different ways of protecting themselves against feeling hurt, the things that make themselves feel good about themselves and the things that mean a lot to them. Ask the children to write, paint, draw or find images to build up their own personal 'coat of arms'.

The sections are:

Places where I feel safe

People that I trust

Things I most enjoy

I wish?

Once the children have thought about the various sections and have found images or drawn things that represent them, they can then start to decorate their shield. Put out the rest of the craft materials and encourage the children to decorate their shields.

Treasure Box

Treasure Box is a creative activity that helps children and young people consider the things that are important to them.

Workers organise the activity by displaying the materials on tables and encouraging the participants to take part by explaining to them that they can make and decorate a treasure box that is personal to them.

Give out the cardboard jewellery boxes and clay. Participants can be encouraged to make their box into any object. We encouraged the young people to make their treasure boxes into snail shapes, which followed on from the storyboard activity. In this programme the snail symbolises the fact that we carry things that are important to us with us, such as hopes, ambitions, memories and ideals. Material things are not the most important things to our sense of identity.

Once the treasure boxes are completed encourage the participants to decorate them. The workers can then help participants to consider the kinds of items that they can put into their treasure box that reflect their hopes, memories, ambitions and ideals. Such objects could include photographs of important people, small items that remind them of happy times, shells, mementos, a lock of hair from someone close, drawings or notes to your self about important things, an autograph from someone you admire and so on.

Activity Sheets for Session Four:

Sid the Snail Storyboard

Sid the Snail sets off to visit his friend. Suddenly a bird swoops and knocks him down the hill. Sid wakes up in a daze and finds that his shell is missing.

What is he thinking?

What is he feeling?

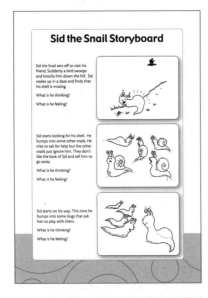

Sid starts looking for his shell. He bumps into some other snails. He tries to ask for help but the other snails just ignore him. They don't like the look of Sid and tell him to go away.

What is he thinking?

What is he feeling?

Sid starts on his way. This time he bumps into some slugs that ask him to play with them.

What is he thinking?

What is he feeling?

One of the slugs realises that Sid is different. They see he has a different coloured body. The slugs laugh at Sid and tell him to go away.

What is he thinking?

What is he feeling?

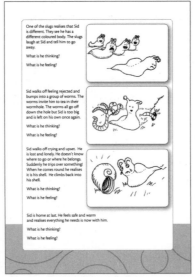

Sid walks off feeling rejected and bumps into a group of worms. The worms invite him to tea in their wormhole. The worms all go off down the hole but Sid is too big and is left on his own once again.

What is he thinking?

What is he feeling?

Sid walks off crying and upset. He is lost and lonely. He doesn't know where to go or where he belongs. Suddenly he trips over something! When he comes round he realises it is his shell. He climbs back into his shell.

What is he thinking?

What is he feeling?

Sid is home at last. He feels safe and warm and realises everything he needs is now with him.

What is he thinking?

What is he feeling?

Sid Loses His Shell

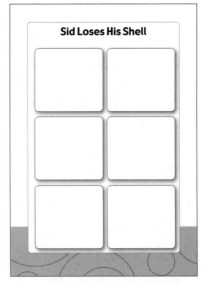

Maisy Loses Her Home Storyboard

Maisy is woken by her mum. The rain hasn't stopped for hours and their home is beginning to flood. 'You need to wake up. We have to leave Maisy, just take what you really need,' says mum.

What is she thinking?

What is she feeling?

List all the things you would take if you were Maisy.

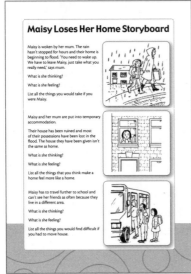

Maisy and her mum are put into temporary accommodation.

Their house has been ruined and most of their possessions have been lost in the flood. The house they have been given isn't the same as home.

What is she thinking?

What is she feeling?

List all the things that you think make a home feel more like a home.

Maisy has to travel further to school and can't see her friends as often because they live in a different area.

What is she thinking?

What is she feeling?

List all the things you would find difficult if you had to move house.

Maisy notices that there are other young people living around her. She gets invited to another young person's house who lives next door.

What is she thinking?

What is she feeling?

List all the things that would make things easier for you if you moved to a new place

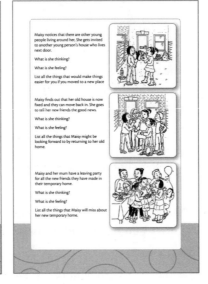

Maisy finds out that her old house is now fixed and they can move back in. She goes to tell her new friends the good news.

What is she thinking?

What is she feeling?

List all the things that Maisy might be looking forward to by returning to her old home.

Maisy and her mum have a leaving party for all the new friends they have made in their temporary home.

What is she thinking?

What is she feeling?

List all the things that Maisy will miss about her new temporary home.

The Day I Lost My Home

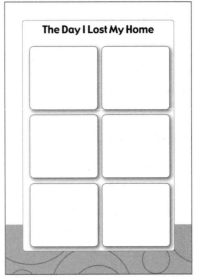

This Is My Shield

It will protect me inside.

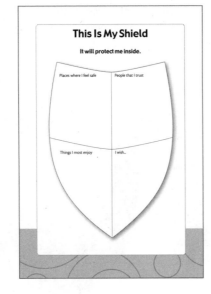

Places where I feel safe

People that I trust

Things I most enjoy

I wish...

Word Association Cards

Love	Hate
Work	Distrust
Future	Wish
Mum	Angry
Home	Hope
Past	Dad
School	Favourite
Scared	Present
Overcome	Play
Hopeless	Best

Resources for Learning Mentors

Programme 2

Just for Lads

Activities to promote resilience and self-esteem in white working class boys

Contents

Foreword by Ian Warwick

Introduction

Session 1: Opening the Group

Session 2: Exploring our feelings about who we are

Session 3: Role Models

Session 4: Poetry and Painting

Session 5: Agony Aunt

Session 6: Hopes, Fears and Dreams

On the CD-ROM

○ Evaluation

○ 12 x Photographs

○ Introducing Me

○ 12 x Biographies

○ Systems of Support

○ Examples of Actions That Can Raise or Lower Self-esteem

○ Definitions of Self-esteem

○ Word Association Cards

○ 6 x Poems

○ 4 x Case Studies

○ Family

○ Friend

○ Teacher

○ Future Lifeline

○ Option Cards

Foreword

Back in 1973 Bernstein argued that:

> We must ensure the material conditions of the school we offer, their values, social organisation, forms of control and pedagogy, the skills and sensitivities of the teachers are refracted through an understanding of the culture the children bring to the school. After all we do no less for the middle class child (p.175).

Unfortunately Bernstein's words seem to have even greater relevance in today's schools.

Boys are four times more likely to be excluded from school and the exclusions are predominantly amongst working class boys, both black and white. Kane (2004) explores some of the reasons for the high rate of exclusions amongst working class boys and highlights a number of key areas, especially the issue of masculinity:

> Some pupils, no matter what schools do, seem to 'kick against' the prevailing school norms, sometimes with overt displays of particular and very challenging forms of masculinities.

For white working class boys their identity has become increasingly confused in a modern world where they are no longer needed to fill the armies of miners, steelworkers, dockers, car plant workers, trawlermen etc. of their father's and grandfather's generations. Instead there are call centres, malls and fast food outlets where the factories once stood.

Nayak (2001) argues that, 'white working class young men have the strongest sense that their masculinities are under siege, which goes some way to explain their defensiveness.'

One of the greatest challenges for schools in recent years has been to respond appropriately to the disillusionment young working class men experience that permeates down to their younger siblings and neighbours.

Reay (2002) suggests we need to face up to the challenge in ways that are more diverse than the simple confrontational response of exclusions and find alternative methods of engaging with boys:

> Until social processes of male gender socialisation move away from privileging the masculine and allow boys to stay in touch with their feminine qualities, the problem of 'failing boys' will remain despite the best efforts of teachers and researchers.

Pamela Allen's work is an excellent response to the challenge of engaging white working class boys and offers ways for schools to engage with a frequently disaffected group of pupils. More importantly it offers an opportunity for the boys themselves to explore their feelings about their environment, their peers and themselves in a way that means they will be better equipped to confront their problems both now and in the future.

Ian Warwick

Introduction

This programme took place over a period of six weeks. The sessions were developed in response to a request to carry out some group work with Year 7 children who were exhibiting challenging behaviour in a comprehensive school.

The rationale for promoting resilience and self-esteem and working preventatively with working class white boys is in response to the prevalence of mental health disorders amongst boys in comparison to girls in all age groups (DOH 2004). Additional risk factors for mental health disorder include family characteristics such as lone parent families, parental unemployment and poor parental education. In addition the suicide rate amongst young men in Britain rose sharply in the 1980s and 1990s, whilst rates for young women have remained relatively stable. Although there has been some decrease in male suicides in recent years the high figures remain a serious concern. In education, boys aged 11-16 are twice as likely to be unhappy and disillusioned at school than girls (Lloyd, 1997). Other external social changes that have had an impact on the lives of young men include the breakdown of traditional gender roles and the shrinkage of traditional manufacturing jobs. Such external changes are likely to impact on the internal mindset set of young men, who are still offered rigid constructions of masculinity, therefore causing conflict (Lloyd, 1997).

Five building blocks of self-esteem

▶ Security - feeling comfortable and safe, knowing what is expected, understanding rules and limits.

▶ Selfhood - acquiring self-knowledge and awareness of individuality.

▶ Affiliation - developing a sense of belonging, feeling appreciated and respected by others.

▶ Mission - having a sense of purpose and motivation in life, taking responsibility for oneself.

▶ Competence - feeling successful in those things considered important, having awareness of strengths and acceptance of weaknesses. (Borba, 2001)

Each of these building blocks were reflected in the materials used during this intervention.

Resilience can be defined as 'normal development under difficult conditions' (Fonagy et al 1994). The fundamental building blocks for resilience are outlined by Gilligan (1997) as:

▶ a secure base

▶ good self-esteem

▶ a sense of self-efficacy.

The participants were identified by the teacher managing the behaviour support unit based on his perceptions of pupils most in need of this support. For the introductory session a group of ten Year 7 pupils arrived, a few on the basis of refusing to attend mainstream lessons and a wish to remain in the behaviour support unit. After some confusion on the first session of who should and should not attend the group, during the next five sessions the group remained relatively stable with the exception of one pupil having a fixed term exclusion from school.

Anticipation of the nature of the emotional and behavioural difficulties experienced by the pupils to be involved in the group made it necessary to plan for positive behaviour management during the sessions. It was decided to use a raffle ticket system where pupils would receive raffle tickets for positive behaviour, such as listening well to others or contributing well to activities, and the raffle would be drawn at the end of each session with the winner receiving a small prize.

Learning from the pilot

▸ The initial planning of the sessions and communication between school staff and outside agencies delivering the programme could be improved, particularly over the selection of pupils to be involved.

▸ The school needs to ensure that parental permission is obtained for all pupils before commencing the programme.

▸ The location of the sessions was important to both adults leading the sessions and the pupils taking part. The room needed to be suitable for both group work and practical activities, in terms of both space and resources. The room used on this occasion was next to the behaviour support unit and therefore other pupils interrupted the group at times.

▸ The timing of the sessions was difficult to manage, as it followed on from break time. Pupils were therefore sometimes late for sessions leading to time management problems within the session.

▸ The activities within the sessions were accessible for the group but adult support was needed for some pupils at times. The range of abilities within the group emphasised the need for differentiation within the activities and tasks. Possible strategies could include alternative recording methods, increased adult support and the opportunity for verbal contributions for those pupils with poor literacy skills.

▸ Positive behaviour management strategies such as the raffle ticket system used during these sessions need to be maintained with more consistency. It may be useful to have one adult in the room to monitor behaviour, give positive feedback to pupils and ensure fairness.

It may also be possible to use this programme in conjunction with the Primary National Strategy Social and Emotional Aspect of Learning (SEAL) in future. The pre-intervention questionnaire for pupils contained within the SEAL materials may be particularly valuable as a measure of suitability of pupils for inclusion in the programme and to assess any changes in behaviour or attitude.

The programme was also piloted in Chaucer school with support from the school nurse Marissa Palmer. The boys selected for the programme by the school were Year 8 pupils with a range of issues and behaviour problems. During this pilot behaviour management methods did not need to be employed and this meant that the focus was much more on the resources and activities. The comments from the school were positive and they felt that the boys engaged with the work positively. The activities they found particularly successful included the images of boys and men and discussing assumptions, the role models and the future career line and they were particularly surprised with how well the pupils engaged with the poetry activity and the standard of work produced. The evaluations from the participants were positive, with 85% rating enjoyment at 7 or above for the sessions and 76% rating learning at 7 or above.

Pamela Allen and Cathy Charles (Educational Psychologist)

Session One

Opening the Group

Aim

To raise awareness of needs and responsibilities when working with others and to facilitate participants' getting to know one another.

Overview

▸ Introduction of facilitators and participants

▸ Introduction of the aims of the groupwork programme

▸ Ground rules and confidentiality.

Materials

▸ Flip chart and pens

▸ Badge making equipment

▸ Coloured pens

▸ Evaluation sheets.

Introduction

It is important to clearly state the aims of the sessions. The underlying theme of this project is to raise self-esteem and resilience in young people. This initial session is the most important in helping the young people understand the benefits of being involved such as: gaining confidence and self-esteem, helping build resilience, developing strategies for coping and support, raising academic aspirations and achievements and developing relationship building skills.

Ice breaker

Name game

In a round each participant and facilitator introduces him or herself and states something that they remember about their given name or that reflects their name. It may be the meaning of the name or a story about how the name was chosen.

Badge making session

All of the participants should write their names and draw a design on a label or a badge and wear it in the session. You can hire badge-making equipment or you can buy badge kits, similar to those used at conferences. If this is too expensive for your budget you can use sticky labels. It does help if the badges are worn for at least the first two or three sessions to help everyone to learn each other's name.

Ground rules

Ask for a volunteer to write down all the ideas and suggestions that the group come up with onto flip chart paper.

All group members participate in developing the rules for the group, for example:

▸ respecting each other

▸ listening to each other

▸ what to do if someone doesn't turn up

▸ being on time

Programme 2

- having the right to not know

- the right to make mistakes.

Trust game

Who am I?

Write a famous person or character's name on a piece of paper and sellotape it onto the back of one of the participants. The participant asks questions to the rest of the group to try to determine who they are. For example, 'Am I a footballer?' The participant continues to ask questions until he guesses the right answer. Below is a list of suggested names that you can use in the activity. Please feel free to add to the list or ask participants themselves to come up with some ideas.

- Bart Simpson

- Eddie Izzard

- Homer Simpson

- David Beckham

- Peter Kay

- Steven Gerrard.

Evaluation

Hand out evaluation sheets to each young person to fill in for the session. Encourage the young people to reflect on the session. Answer any questions participants may have about the group. Mention briefly what the contents of the following week's session will contain.

Session Two

Exploring Our Feelings About Who We Are

Aim

To promote awareness about internal and external factors that influence the way we perceive ourselves.

Overview

▸ An introduction to concepts about how we see ourselves in the world, our likes and dislikes

▸ An exploration of how society might judge us because of our looks, our image, our culture, etc.

Materials

▸ Polaroid camera and film

▸ A4 sheets of paper x 2

▸ Images of mean and boys

▸ Pens, glue stick, flip chart paper

▸ 'Introducing me' form

▸ Blank index cards

▸ Evaluation sheets.

Check in

▸ Welcome participants back to the group and ask if they have had any thoughts about the last session.

▸ Reintroduce the ground rules and ask participants if they have anything to add.

Ice breaker

I am

Hand out a sheet of A4 paper to each participant and ask him to write his name at the top.

Ask the participants to write out the statement 'I am' and then use five different statements that will tell the other participants something about himself.

For example, I am:

▸ the oldest child of three

▸ a big fan of football

▸ good at art

▸ keen on sport

▸ a fan of R&B music.

Put the participants into pairs and ask them to introduce each other using the information on the paper.

One partner then introduces his partner to the other members of the group.

Ask the participants how the activity felt and what new things they learned about the other participants.

Introducing Me

Introduce the 'Introducing Me' activity sheets and ask participants to fill in the sheet. Whilst they are filling in the sheet quickly go round and take photographs of the participants. Once the pictures are ready participants can glue their photograph to the sheet.

Definitions/Assumptions

The facilitator shows images of mean and boys doing different things. These photographs are supplied as a full colour A4 printable resource on the accompanying CD-ROM. The images are taken from Male Image Photo Pack, produced by Working With Men (www.workingwithmen.org) and we appreciate their consent to use the material for this programme.

Other images you can use are public school boys, boys participating in various sports and so on.

Ask the participants to brainstorm what they think about these men and boys asking questions such as:

- ▶ What class are they from?
- ▶ What type of family do they live in?
- ▶ What kind of house?
- ▶ Do they have brothers and sisters?
- ▶ What would society think about them?
- ▶ How do they think they will turn out?
- ▶ What do you think they do in their spare time?
- ▶ What kinds of music do you think they would be in to?
- ▶ How do you think they get on at school?
- ▶ What kinds of judgements do you think adults would make about them?

The facilitators encourage discussion and debate on the issues and flipcharts the participant's responses.

Trust game

Knowing me knowing you

The facilitator hands out blank postcards and asks participants to write their name in the centre. The postcards are then passed around the group and each group member writes something they have learnt about the person written in the centre of the postcard. Participants should write one thing that is positive which they have noticed or something they have learnt in the session about that person. When the postcard has been around the circle the completed card should end up back with the named person, with comments from all the other group members. Facilitators need to ensure that only positive comments or observations are made about other group members.

Discuss how it felt to give and receive such comments.

Evaluation

Hand out evaluation forms to each young person to fill in for the session. Encourage the young people to reflect on the session. Answer any questions participants may have about the group. Mention briefly what the contents of the following week's session will contain.

Activity Sheets for Session Two:

1 of 12 on the CD-ROM

Session Three

Role Models

Aim

To introduce positive role models. To begin thinking about systems of support that young people can utilise in dealing with life's adversities.

Overview

An introduction to white working class male role models from their local area and around the world that have contributed to society and made successful achievements in their lives.

An introduction to the notion of self-esteem and how feelings of worth can be affected by internal coping strategies as well as other people's attitudes and behaviour towards us.

Materials

- ▸ Extracts of autobiographies of role models. These can be enhanced with photographs or pictures from magazines, or from website searches.
- ▸ Flip chart, paper, pens
- ▸ Examples of actions
- ▸ Definition of self-esteem
- ▸ List of systems of support available
- ▸ Evaluation sheets.

Check in

Welcome back to group. Ask participants if they have had any thoughts about the group since last week, and what they took away from last week's session.

Ice breaker

Positive comments

Ask participants to sit in two lines facing each other. Each participant in turn then makes a positive comment about the person sitting opposite. It may be better for the facilitator to start the process unless a participant volunteers. Comments could be related to the way the person looks or their characteristics, for example, 'I think you are kind' and so on.

Role models

The facilitator introduces an example of a positive role model with a brief description of their journey and achievements. It may be worth spending some time finding local famous role models, images and autobiographies from the Internet, with which the participating lads can identify. The published programme was piloted in Sheffield and therefore there are a number of biographies of Sheffield role models. By choosing local figures it is possible to highlight the ethos of the programme and to ground it in working class history, culture and identity. The autobiographies can be printed from the CD-ROM and enhanced with pictures from various sources. The participants choose a role model out of the remaining examples and reads out the description to the other participants. The participants then work on their own to answer three questions in relation to the role model they have chosen. (It may be better for the facilitator to give a brief overview of all the role models in the pack so that those participants who have limited reading skills are not excluded):

1. How did the role model become famous?

2. What was their background, where did they come from?

3. In what way does this person inspire you, what do you like about this person?

Once the participants have completed their answers ask them to share their answers with the rest of the group commenting on any similarities and differences about why they chose the role model they did. You can ask the participants if they have their own examples of positive role models that they could share with the group.

Support

Ask participants to brainstorm what qualities and support the role models needed in order to become successful. What is it about the person and what help did they need to get where they got?

The facilitator writes on flipchart paper the ideas participants present, splitting the responses into internal personal qualities and external support factors.

Show participants the list of different types of support systems that are available.

Discuss with the participants their knowledge of different services that offer support and whether they have any knowledge about how to access such support.

What do I do to make people feel good or bad about themselves?

The facilitator splits the participants into two groups: one group to think about the 'Good' things people do or say to make others feel good and the other group to think about 'Bad' things people do or say that has the potential for making us feel bad about ourselves. It is better if the facilitator gives a few examples to start the process.

Ask each group to write down their ideas on flip chart and feed back to the whole group once they have finished.

The facilitator introduces the notion that self-esteem can be strongly affected by how people are treated and then go through the examples of actions to see if there where any others that the group did not come up with.

The facilitator reads out the definitions of self-esteem and asks for any comments from the group.

Discuss with the group if they can think of anything else that may impact on how we view our self worth.

Evaluation

Hand out evaluation forms to each young person to fill in for the session. Encourage the young people to reflect on the session. Answer any questions participants may have about the group. Mention briefly what the contents of the following week's session will contain.

Activity Sheets for Session Three:

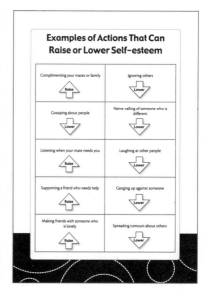

1 of 12 on the CD-ROM

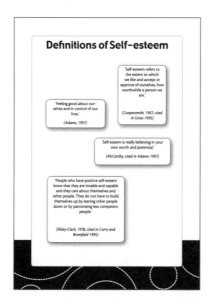

Programme 2

Session Four

Poetry and Painting

Aim

To explore alternative media to express our feelings and thoughts about our identity, class, masculinity and future hopes.

Overview

Participants use poetry and prose, painting and visualisation to discover ways to express their personal stories.

Materials

- Examples of poetry from working class white males
- Paints, brushes, palettes, paper, pens
- Role model autobiographies
- Guided imagery script
- Blank postcards
- Evaluation sheets.

Check in

Welcome back to the group.

Ask if participants have had any thoughts about the session from the week before.

Ice breaker

Who is it?

Hand out blank postcards and pens to each participant. Each participant then writes a statement about themsleves on the card that they think no one else in the group will know about him, for example, a hobby, future plans, an achievement that they are proud of and so on.

When all the group members have finished the postcards, place them face down in the middle of the group.

In turn participants pick a card and try to guess who has written it. The participant keeps guessing until they get it right. If the participant picks up their own card or one that has already been read out, they pick again and the cards get reshuffled.

Poetry

Help participants to reflect back about the autobiographies of role models from the week before and ask the participants to think about how these individuals overcame barriers to be successful.

The facilitator reads out examples of poetry written about working class issues, adolescence or issues of identity. There are a number of poems that participants have written within the pack that you can use as examples. Other poetry or songs that were used in the group included *Working Class Hero* by John Lennon, *Wicked World* by Benjamin Zephaniah, *Missing, Formerly Antony Arnold*, by Antony Arnold, *The Leader* by Roger McGough and *Survivor* by Roger McGough. You can use any poetry or prose that you think is relevant to working class or male identify. Once you have read out the poetry of your choice give out poetry paper and pens.

Ask the participants to think about their own personal experiences and ask them to write down a poem, rap or prose that reflects those experiences. The word association cards may help to stimulate ideas for some participants.

Once the participants have written their poems, prose or rap ask if anyone would like to share what he has written.

If writing is an issue and you have access to a tape recorder ask the participants to record their poem, rap or prose onto the tape provided.

Guided imagery

Discovering our inner strength

Before reading out the guided imagery ensure that the paper and materials have been put out before the visualisation so that participants can begin immediately drawing and painting without interruption.

Arrange the activity in a quiet space and ensure that there are no interruptions. Ask participants to sit or lie down and read out the guided imagery script. After the relaxation exercise participants can then paint or draw the image of their special place.

If the facilities do not allow for painting or drawing, discuss with the participants their experience of the relaxation exercise. It is often useful to point out that sports celebrities, actors and other people who want to perform at their peak often use relaxation techniques to help them to stay focused and calm.

Evaluation

Hand out evaluation forms to each young person to fill in for the session. Encourage the young people to reflect on the session. Answer any questions participants may have about the group. Mention briefly what the contents of the following week's session will contain.

A letter by Brendan
I used to be very bad
And got a lot of clips off my dad
But then that made me mad
Five days later
I killed my dad
But that made me sad
I've learnt my lesson
I feel very sad
This is my last letter
I will be killed by my dad
Thanks for listening
I am still very bad

Football

I would love to be a footballer
For Rotherham United.
I would like to score a goal
At Old Trafford.
I would hate to lose
In the Champions League Final.
I would hate to score an own goal.
And the best thing of all
Is going to sleep in my bed.
Goodbye.
Ryan

Limo

Big car flashing
Inside music
Blasting, Booming
In it for one hour
Drinking, bower
That's that crazy
Limo hour by the
Hour
Perry

Empty Head

My head is empty,
I cannot think
I'm under pressure
I just can't think
I wish I was different
I want to be big
Instead of this smallness
Of life in the sticks
My head is empty
I cannot think
I'm under pressure
Life just stinks
Aaron

I would

I would love to be motor bike rider
I would like to have big house
And I am sometimes bad in school
But I always try hard
I would love to work as a builder on houses
I would like to have a KX 250cc
Liam

Tired, Tired, Tired

Falling out of trees
Five years old
Playing Batman
Running across the road
No cars to be seen
My dad's best friend
Deer trapped in the lights
Lights went to the back of my head
I was in shock
I felt nothing
The only thing I feel
Is going to sleep
All I see in front of me is
Raffle tickets
All I feel is
Tired, tired, tired
I am now bored of my life
Because the worst thing I have done is
Put my hand through a window when I was 10.

Aaron

Resources for Learning Mentors

Activity Sheets for Session Four:

Discovering Our Inner Strength

Find a space and get as comfortable as you can. So that you can really relax and enjoy this, take some deep breaths – very quietly so no-one else can hear. Draw the breath in, hold it and then slowly release it.

Do this several times. Check your body, your arms and legs, everywhere, to see if you can feel any tension. If you can, send some relaxing breath to that place. When you are ready, close your eyes and start to enjoy the feeling of going on a journey in your imagination.

It starts with you in a field. The grass is just as you like it, there are some flowers growing in it and perhaps some little animals scurrying around and going about their business. You are enjoying being there, the sun is shining and everything is fine. You can see a path which leads into some woods. Walk along it, perhaps kicking the leaves as you go or looking out for rabbits or squirrels. As you go further you realise that the wood is at the bottom of a mountain. You decide to climb it and you are soon on an open path going upwards. It gets quite steep, but that doesn't stop you. You have plenty of energy and now you are determined to reach the top. There are easy parts, there are rocky places.

Your legs are working hard, you breathe deeply and feel strong. You go on and on, up and up, until finally at last you are there. You find that it is a really beautiful place and you are pleased to have reached it...(pause)

Sitting there already you see a young person who waves and smiles at you. You both move to meet and greet each other. Soon you are talking and playing together as if you have been friends for a long time. You know that this person is special to you and will always be your friend. You know you can talk about anything with your friend and you will always get help and support and good company. If there are any questions you want to ask, you will always get the answer...(pause).

You really enjoy being with your friend and doing the things you both like doing. You have more fun than you've ever had...(pause)

Now it's time to leave. Your friend says you can come back at any time and you say you will visit often. You say good-bye and go back down the path and through the woods feeling very pleased to have met your friend and to know you can return whenever you want.

The path leads you through the field and comes to the entrance to this building. You walk through and into the building and into this room. Have a stretch and yawn.

Open your eyes gently and when you are ready come back into the circle.

Spend time drawing or writing about your experience.

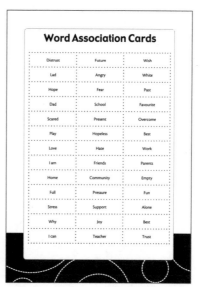

Word Association Cards

Distrust	Future	Wish
Lad	Angry	White
Hope	Fear	Past
Dad	School	Favourite
Scared	Present	Overcome
Play	Hopeless	Best
Love	Hate	Work
I am	Friends	Parents
Home	Community	Empty
Full	Pressure	Fun
Stress	Support	Alone
Why	Joy	Best
I can	Teacher	Trust

Session Five

Agony Aunt

Aim

To explore transgenerational, cultural and personal issues that young people may encounter.

Overview

Using case studies or scenarios of problem situations participants think about what support may be available to address some of the difficulties highlighted.

Material

> ▸ Case studies

> ▸ Formatted paper available as a printable resource on CD-ROM

> ▸ List of systems of support available

> ▸ Evaluation sheets.

Check in

Welcome participants back to the group and ask if they have any questions, thoughts about last week's session.

Ice breaker

The rule of the game

A volunteer is chosen to leave the room. Explain to the participants that you would like them to decide what is to be the rule of the game. Rules can include such things as, answering with your feet off the ground, crossing or uncrossing your legs while answering, giving an answer starting with the same letter of the alphabet as your own name and so on. The person outside is recalled. The chosen person then asks the rest of the participant's questions. Listening and watching carefully for the answers they have to try and guess the rule.

Case studies

Split the group into sets of threes and give each group a case study. Each group then picks different formatted paper, which will determine whether they are:

1. A friend.

2. A teacher.

3. A family member.

The participants write their responses to the case study in the role that they have chosen.

Bring the group back together and ask the participants to read out their responses to the case studies.

Discuss the kinds of support that they have thought of. Look at the list of systems of support available and ask if any of the ones they did not mention would also be useful to the young person in the scenario. Discuss with the participants the differences and similarities in the advice that they gave. Check whether this was determined by the problem of the young person in the scenario or whether it was determined by their role as advisor. Explore the fact that some issues are easier to solve than others. Explain that when there are lots of external factors such as poverty, racism, loss and isolation, issues can become very complex to sort out on your own. Explain that external support and help or advocacy may be necessary to prevent problems becoming even worse.

Trust game

The pride line

In a round each participant to finish the sentence, 'I am proud that...' Some examples may be: things that you have done for your parents, things you have done for a friend, things you have done for yourself, things you have made, how you spend your free time, habits you have, some thing you have tried hard for, how you have earned some money, something you believe in, a new skill you have acquired, the nicest thing you have done for someone in the last week.

Evaluation

Hand out evaluation forms to each young person to fill in for the session. Encourage the young people to reflect on the session. Answer any questions participants may have about the group. Mention briefly what the contents of the following week's session will contain.

Activity Sheets for Session Five:

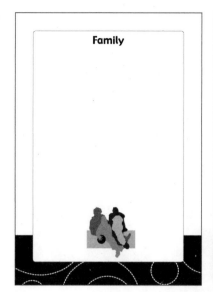

Family

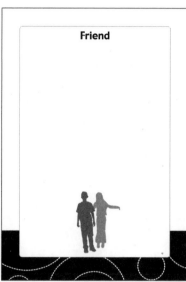

Friend

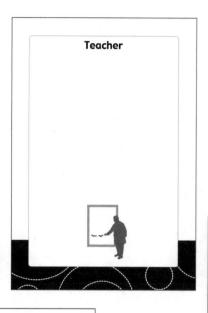

Teacher

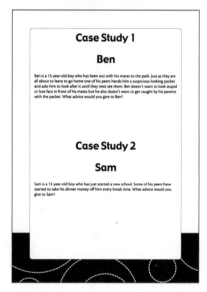

Case Study 1

Ben

Ben is a 13-year-old boy who has been out with his mates to the park. Just as they are all about to leave to go home one of his peers hands him a suspicious looking packet and asks him to look after it until they next see them. Ben doesn't want to look stupid or lose face in front of his mates but he also doesn't want to get caught by his parents with the packet. What advice would you give to Ben?

Case Study 2

Sam

Sam is a 12-year-old boy who has just started a new school. Some of his peers have started to take his dinner money off him every break time. What advice would you give to Sam?

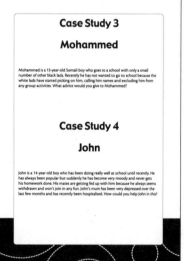

Case Study 3

Mohammed

Mohammed is a 13-year-old Somali boy who goes to a school with only a small number of other black lads. Recently he has not wanted to go to school because the white lads have started picking on him, calling him names and excluding him from any group activities. What advice would you give to Mohammed?

Case Study 4

John

John is a 14-year-old boy who has been doing really well at school until recently. He has always been popular but suddenly he has become very moody and never gets his homework done. His mates are getting fed up with him because he always seems withdrawn and won't join in any fun. John's mum has been very depressed over the last few months and has recently been hospitalised. How could you help John in this?

Session Six

Hopes, Fears and Dreams

Aim

To explore individual aspirations and hopes for the future. To consider realistic options and to look at what they will need to start doing in order to achieve their goals.

Overview

Participants run through exercises that help them plan for the future, using a career lifeline to explore their options.

Materials

- Career lifeline
- Option cards
- Flip chart paper, pens
- Ball of string or wool
- Scissors
- Certificates
- Evaluation sheets.

Check in

Welcome back to the group. Give participants time to raise any issues they have from last week's session.

Ice breaker

The best thing that happened to me this week

In a round each participant finishes off the statement:

'The best thing that happened to me this week was...'

It can be followed by different rounds, such as:

'If I had this week to live over what I would change is...'

'If I was a famous person I would be...'

'I'd like to write a book about...'

'If I were an animal I would be a...'

'Some things I want to do before I die are...' and so on.

Hopes, fears and dreams

Give a piece of flipchart paper out to each participant with 'Hopes', 'Fears' and 'Dreams' written on and ask them to brainstorm their own hopes, fears and dreams for the future.

Participants share with the group some of their ideas. Discuss any issues that arise, for example difficulty of looking into the future if you do not know where you are going to be living in the next few months. Having realistic expectations when the media and television are full of people who seem to have lots of material possessions and attention but do not seem to have worked hard to achieve such status.

Programme 2

Future lifeline

Give out the 'Future Lifeline' activity sheet printed onto A3 paper and give a set of Option Cards to each participant. Leave some of the Option Cards blank so that they can choose their own ideas. Ask participants to fill in the lifeline individually.

Help the participants think about where they would like to be heading: career, college, being a parent and so on. The participants should share with the group some of their options and, if there are gaps in the lifeline, discuss what the blocks may be to making decisions, for example, is it too far ahead to think about?

Ask participants to brainstorm things that help achieve goals and write them on flipchart paper, for example, personal skills, Connexions, research on the internet, attending careers fairs, support from family, determination, being allowed to make decisions, encouragement from teachers, confidence, being allowed to make mistakes, being allowed to have fun.

Trust game

Saying goodbye

Ask participants to sit in a circle with one member holding a ball of string or wool.

The participant with the ball looks around and says a goodbye and a final message to one of the other participants. Holding on to the end of the string/wool they throw the ball to the participant they said the goodbye to.

The person who receives the ball then repeats the process.

This carries on until the process comes to a natural end.

At the end there is silence and the facilitator then cuts all the string that is now criss-crossing the circle, symbolising the end of the group.

Evaluation

Hand out evaluation forms to each young person to fill in for the session. Encourage the young people to reflect on the session. Answer any questions participants may have about the group.

Activity Sheets for Session Six:

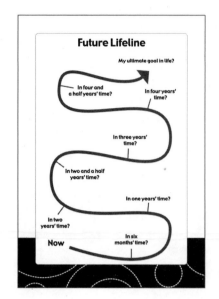

Future Lifeline

My ultimate goal in life?

In four and a half years' time?

In four years' time?

In three years' time?

In two and a half years' time?

In one years' time?

In two years' time?

In six months' time?

Now

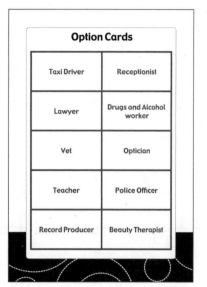

Option Cards

Taxi Driver	Receptionist
Lawyer	Drugs and Alcohol worker
Vet	Optician
Teacher	Police Officer
Record Producer	Beauty Therapist

Programme 3

Girls' Own

Activities to promote self-esteem, assertiveness and resilience

Developed in collaboration with Vicki Ransom and Rebecca Allard from Fir Vale School

Contents

Foreword by Liz Johnson

Introduction

Session 1: Opening the group

Session 2: Relationships

Session 3: Self-esteem

Session 4: Assertiveness

Session 5: Stress and Relaxation

Session 6: Hopes, Fears and Dreams

On the CD-ROM

○ Evaluation Sheet

○ Introducing Me

○ Different Relationships We May Have

○ Why Do Young People Have Relationships?

○ Examples of Actions that Can Raise or Lower Self-esteem

○ Definitions of Self-esteem

○ Agony Aunt

○ Challenge These Statements

○ Challenge These Statements (some possible answers)

○ What Is Assertiveness?

○ Role Play Scenario

○ Aggressive Behaviour

○ Passive Behaviour

○ Indirect Behaviour

○ Assertive Behaviour

○ Situation Cards

○ Stilling Script

○ Body Language

○ Assertiveness Skills Sheet

○ Assertiveness Quiz

○ 3 x Pictures

○ Body

○ Physical Symptoms of Stress

○ Tips to Beat Stress

○ Guided Fantasy: Beach/Cloud

○ Guided Fantasy: Magic Carpet

○ General Relaxation

○ Progressive Muscle Relaxation

○ Going on a Trip

○ Future Lifeline

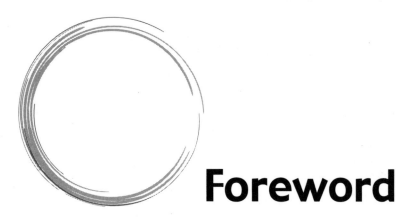

Foreword

The *Youth Matters* Green Paper (July 2005) highlights the link between good emotional and physical health and success in learning while *Making It Possible: Improving Mental Health and Wellbeing in England* (2005) includes principles such as valuing yourself and others, talking about your feelings, keeping in touch with friends, getting involved and making a contribution, and asking for help. Building strong foundations to achieve these objectives through initiatives focused on supporting young people are essential. These principles underpin the current preventative approach of developing good mental health through attention to emotional wellbeing, as well as tackling issues related to the prevention of social exclusion, which may develop as a result of poor mental health. In order to work, maintain social relationships and take part in leisure and other opportunities, individuals require confidence and a reasonable level of self-esteem and their ability to engage in these areas in turn has a positive impact on a person's mental wellbeing.

The Social Exclusion Unit report *Mental Health and Social Exclusion* (June 2004) describes the ways in which poor mental health can lead to, 'a vicious cycle of social exclusion, including unemployment, debt, homelessness and worsening health.' However it is also clear in stating that, 'breaking the cycle requires a focus on early intervention, and fulfilling people's aspirations and potential through work and social participation.' Even short-term common mental health problems can have a significant impact on the individual, with the consequent risk of the development of social exclusion. Therefore ne of the key ways of tackling this issue is to work on ways of preventing poor mental health from developing in the first place.

It is important that everyone looks after their personal mental health in the same way that they look after their physical health; however in the same way that certain groups of people are more vulnerable to suffering poor physical health it is also the case that women are particularly vulnerable to suffering from certain types of mental health problems. *Mainstreaming Gender and Women's Mental Health Services* (DoH 2003) highlights the fact that, 'many causes of women's mental ill health, and failure to manage them in the community, lie in their social environment, including poverty, sexism, racism, housing, parenting and family issues, violence and abuse.' It also states that, 'these can often be influenced by public health measures that offer support and early intervention for vulnerable women and communities.' It is clear therefore that any preventive interventions targeted at promoting confidence and positive mental health in young women will assist their resilience to factors within their environment that are often beyond their direct control.

The 'Girls' Own' project concentrates on the development and maintenance of emotional wellbeing and confidence, therefore recognising the significance of mental health wellbeing promotion, while also recognising the significance of attention to gender specific factors in addressing these issues.

Liz Johnson

Acting Head of Patient Experience, Social Inclusion and Diversity - Sheffield Care Trust

Introduction

Research has identified many advantages of joint working between Child and Adolescent Mental Health Services and schools and such work enables access to children who may not normally be reached. The Mental Health Foundation (Pettitt. 2003) found that school staff reported an increase in children's happiness, wellbeing and behaviour and some workers reported links to improved academic attainment.

Research also suggests that young people, predominantly girls, experience a decline in self-esteem as they enter their adolescent years (Bower, 2004). During adolescence, girls show a decline in instrumental characteristics (less assertive, less self-confident and have lower expectations regarding their ability to control important events), which leads them to feel less confident in their ability to solve problems. It is these attributes which have been shown to make girls more vulnerable to depression in adolescence (Marcotte, 1999). Gilligan (1990) believes that girls learn best and gain increased self-confidence through collaboration with others and not through competition with others as practised in most schools. In response to the issues that surround adolescent girls and the school's desire to support these particular pupils a preventative, resilience building groupwork programme was developed. Smithers (2006) wrote an article about girls' groups and tackling low self-esteem by allowing girls space to talk. One participant said, 'This has made me feel normal. I like the fact that the teachers take part with you and you feel you can really talk to them. They are mums as well as teachers and they talk about their own lives. The things I was worried about, I have found everyone worries about. The club has definitely given me more confidence.'

The programme has been piloted in two schools in Sheffield. Both schools were encouraged to think carefully about the participants for the group. One school decided on a group of girls who were bright, articulate and well-motivated. The school wanted to explore different strategies to deal with conflict that they had not previously tried. They decided to use older girls as role models for Year 8 pupils that were of similar ability but were also experiencing conflict.

The other school decided on a group of Year 8 pupils with a range of needs from multiple losses, difficulties at home of varying degrees, self-harm, concerns around behaviour, relationship issues, lack of assertion and low self-esteem.

One of the aims of the collaboration was to enable the schools to develop a larger repertoire to deal with issues in a positive way and to leave them feeling confident to run the programme on their own in the future.

This project was a positive experience for everyone taking part.

Comments from the staff who participated in the project included:

▸ Excellent atmosphere throughout the course.

▸ Positive response from the pupils.

▸ Good to work with external agency collaboratively.

▸ Positive relationships formed between year groups.

▸ Positive relationships formed between the group members that would not have been formed if they had not shared the group process.

▸ Good use of resources.

▸ Thought provoking exercises that the students could go away and discuss at the next meeting.

▸ The course helped them to see that they were not alone and that they had shared ideas and interests.

▸ The work has increased participants' esteem and confidence.

▸ The programme can be used to work with other girls.

- Changes in the participants are already being noted in their ability to cope and be more resilient and that there has been a marked improvement in peer relationships and friendships.

- Can adapt and use the resources in the groupwork in one to one situations.

They also suggested areas for improvement:

- One member of staff did not have enough time to join all the workshops with the new workload.

- The school setting was often unpredictable, especially in the learning support unit where there were often vulnerable children. This needs to be taken into consideration when planning the work as members of staff may have to be removed at short notice. Space was often at a premium and having a consistent venue can prove challenging.

- Evaluations to be filled in by the students at the correct time.

Overall comments from the young people included:

'All the sessions made sense in the end. Even the bits that were boring, and when we did the relaxation, it sounded daft but it worked.'

'We learnt new things that we thought were silly, but it worked.'

'I enjoyed making new friends.'

'The best bit for me was meeting new people and learning new things such as respecting your body and being self-confident.'

'I thought it was good because you got to find out you were not alone and other people think like you.'

'I enjoyed the relaxation and calming you down.'

'I really enjoyed learning all about relationships.'

'I learned about controlling my own emotions and how they affect other people.'

'It gave me a chance to share problems and get higher self-esteem.'

'It was a chance to talk.'

'A chance to understand others' feelings.'

'It raised my confidence, and knowing how to build new friendships and to join in more in other lessons and classes.'

'We all really trust each other now in the group and would turn to each other for help and we know that we would help each other.'

'The positive strokes activity made us feel nice inside and made us happy and I felt that other people did like me.'

Session One

Opening the Group

Aim

To raise awareness of needs and responsibilities when working with others and to facilitate participants' getting to know one another.

Overview

- ▸ Introduction of facilitators and participants
- ▸ Introduction of the aims of the groupwork programme
- ▸ Ground rules and confidentiality
- ▸ Introducing Me.

Materials

- ▸ Flipchart and pens
- ▸ Glue stick, pens
- ▸ 'Introducing Me' activity sheet
- ▸ Polaroid camera and film or digital camera
- ▸ Evaluation sheets.

Introduction

It is important to clearly state the aims of the sessions. The underlying theme of this project is to raise self-esteem and resilience in young people. This initial session is the most important in helping the young people understand the benefits of being involved such as gaining confidence and self-esteem, helping build resilience, developing strategies for coping and support, raising academic aspirations and achievements and developing relationship building skills.

Ice breaker

Name game

Ask for a participant to begin a round with their name and then state: 'If I had a thousand pounds I would...' The next participant then says the previous speaker's name, what they would buy with a thousand pounds and adds her own wish. The next participant then has to remember the previous two speaker's names and wishes and add their own and so on until the last person in the round has to memorise all the group participants' names and wishes.

Ground rules

Ask for a participant to volunteer to write the group's ideas onto flip chart paper.

Ask the young people to introduce themselves and say one good quality of a friend that they can think of.

Ask the participants if these qualities could provide the ground rules the group could use to enable them to work together smoothly.

All the group members can then participate in developing the rules for the group. The facilitators may want to add some rules they think might be important to the group, for example:

- ▸ respecting each other
- ▸ listening to each other

- what to do if someone doesn't turn up

- being on time

- having the right to not know or to make mistakes and so on.

Introducing Me

Distribute the 'Introducing Me' activity sheet and ask participants fill it in. While they are filling in the sheet quickly go round and take photographs of the participants. Once the pictures are ready participants can glue their photograph to the sheet. If you have time, participants could take photographs of one another and if you do not have a Polaroid camera you can use a digital camera and print off the photographs for the participants to use the following week.

Evaluation

Hand out evaluation sheets to each young person to fill in for the session. Encourage the young people to reflect on the session. Answer any questions participants may have about the group. Mention briefly what the contents of the following week's session will contain.

Activity Sheet for Session One:

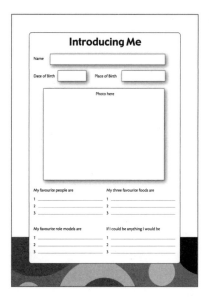

Introducing Me

Name

Date of Birth   Place of Birth

Photo here

My favourite people are
1
2
3

My three favourite foods are
1
2
3

My favourite role models are
1
2
3

If I could be anything I would be
1
2
3

Session Two

Relationships

Aim

To introduce the notion that there are a variety of relationships we develop during our lifetime and how these serve different functions at different times. Relationships play a significant part in our emotional, social and behavioural development. They provide the opportunity to acquire knowledge, develop skills and develop a level of confidence, which allows us to feel positive about ourselves and respect others. The way people conduct their relationships with one another can either help or hinder an individual's own mental and emotional health.

Overview

- ‣ Exploring relationships that are important to us.
- ‣ Introduction to positive and negative relationships and why we have them.
- ‣ Exploring different relationships and what makes them different.
- ‣ Why do young people have relationships?

Materials

- ‣ Flip chart paper, pens
- ‣ Jar of small stones or buttons
- ‣ Images of famous relationships that you have found from magazines or photographs from website searches
- ‣ Scarfs or blindfolds
- ‣ Evaluation sheets.

Check in

Welcome back to group. Ask participants if they have had any thoughts about the group since last week, and what they took away from last week's session.

Ice breaker

Look up, look down

Ask the participants to stand in a circle and look at the ground. On the facilitator's command participants look up and if they look at someone who is also looking at them they then form another circle. The next circle then proceeds in their own circle at the same time as the main circle, looking up and down when the facilitator says. If those in the small circle make eye contact they rejoin the main circle and if anyone in the main circle makes eye contact they join the smaller circle and so on.

Stone therapy

The facilitator introduces the concept of using stones to represent important people in the participants' lives. Ask the participants to choose six stones out of the jar, one of these stones representing themselves. The participants are asked to choose the stone that they feel best represents them and why. This could be to do with the colour, texture, and shape or feeling that they associate with the stone they choose. For example, a participant may choose a stone that has two colours saying that they feel this represents different aspects of their personality. One shade may be more subtle and subdued representing their quiet side and times they want to be more introverted. The other shade may be more vibrant, representing their social and lively side. Once the participants have talked about their own stone ask them to then place their stone in the middle and to place the remaining stones around them.

These stones need to represent important people in their lives. It is best if the facilitator goes first and demonstrates the exercise by using their personal family and relationships. The stones placed closest to the participant's own stone represents those relationships that they feel are the closest to them. For example, as a facilitator you may place your partner and children very close to your own stone and then place your mother or father, brothers, sisters or friends at varying spaces depending on how good you feel that relationship is or how often you keep in touch.

Once the stones have been placed ask participants to explain to the rest of the group who their stones represent and why they have placed them where they have. Once completed ask the participants to choose one stone that they would like to keep and take with them to remind them of that important relationship.

Different relationships

Ask the participants to think about all the various kinds of relationships that people have. Ask if anyone would like to volunteer to be a scribe to write down all the ideas that the group comes out with. These relationships can include short and long term relationships. Ask the participants to comment on their ideas. Are these relationships the same? What makes them different?

Why do young people have relationships?

Ask the participants to think about all the reasons that they seek out relationships with others. Ask for a volunteer scribe to write down all the ideas the group comes up with. Discuss with participants that relationships vary from person to person. What is common to most relationships and what makes them important is that they help us to develop emotionally and socially. All relationships have their ups and downs and it is our ability to overcome the bad times in relationships and understand what is going on for yourself and the other person that helps us to become resilient.

Famous relationships

Ask participants to work in pairs and handout the images of famous people that you have found from magazines or website searches. Famous relationships that were used in the pilot of the groupwork included Sharon Osborne, Louis Walsh and Simon Cowell, Peter Andre and Jordan, Ant and Dec, David and Victoria Beckham and Prince Charles and the Queen. Ask the participants to consider the relationship that these celebrities have. What function does the relationship serve? Does their relationship have the capacity to boost the confidence of the other partner or can it have a damaging consequence? What may get in the way of these relationships being positive? Ask the participants to feed back their ideas to the larger group.

Trust game

Trust in me

Ask the participants to get into pairs. One of the participants has the role of being the guide and the other participant has to close her eyes or put a scarf around her eyes. The guide then leads the blindfolded person around the room and the blindfolded person has to trust the guide to keep them safe. After a few minutes ask the pairs to swap roles and repeat the exercise. Ask the participants how it felt to be guided. Did they feel anxious, worried or relaxed and what made the difference in how they felt?

Evaluation

Hand out evaluation sheets to each young person to fill in for the session. Encourage the young people to reflect on the session. Answer any questions participants may have about the group. Mention briefly what the contents of the following week's session will contain. Inform the participants that they can think about an object that is important to them and if they would like bring it in the next week to share with the group.

Activity Sheets for Session Two:

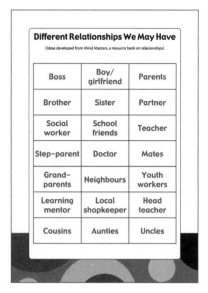

Different Relationships We May Have

(Ideas developed from Mind Matters, a resource bank on relationships)

Boss	Boy/girlfriend	Parents
Brother	Sister	Partner
Social worker	School friends	Teacher
Step-parent	Doctor	Mates
Grand-parents	Neighbours	Youth workers
Learning mentor	Local shopkeeper	Head teacher
Cousins	Aunties	Uncles

Why Do Young People Have Relationships?

(Ideas developed from Mind Matters - a resource bank on relationships)

Healthy

○ To meet new people
○ To share ideas with someone with a similar way of thinking
○ To have fun
○ To belong to something such as a club
○ To learn new things
○ To provide and receive emotional support
○ To avoid being lonely
○ To care and be cared for
○ To understand someone else's point of view
○ To increase self-esteem
○ Because as human beings we are social and need contact with others
○ To develop a sense of self and belonging

Unhealthy

○ To have power over others
○ To be dependant on others
○ To be looked after
○ To have status because the person you are with has status
○ Money
○ To stop yourself being scared or a victim
○ Using others to further your own goals.

Session Three

Self-esteem

Aim

To introduce the notion of self-esteem. To show how feelings of worth can be affected by internal coping strategies as well as other people's attitudes and behaviour towards us.

Overview

- ▸ Consideration of the different actions that can impact on how we feel about ourselves.
- ▸ Raise awareness of what it would feel like to have low self-esteem.
- ▸ Practise giving positive feedback to other group members.

Materials

- ▸ Treasures (such as shells, beads and wood)
- ▸ 'Examples of Actions That Can Raise or Lower Self-esteem' activity sheet
- ▸ 'Definition of Self-esteem' activity sheet
- ▸ 'Problem Page' activity sheet
- ▸ A4 sheets of paper
- ▸ Sellotape
- ▸ Evaluation sheets.

Check in

Welcome back to group. Ask participants if they have had any thoughts about the group since last week, and what they took away from last week's session.

Ice breaker

Treasures

The facilitator lays out different natural objects, such as shells, beads and wood, or ask participants to share with the group an important object that they have bought from home. The facilitator asks participants to choose an object and then share with the group the reason they chose the object, what it represents to them and how it feels etc.

What do I do to make people feel good or bad about themselves?

Split the participants into two groups: one group to think about the 'Good' things people do or say to make others feel good and the other group to think about 'Bad' things people do or say that has the potential for making us feel bad about ourselves. It is better if the facilitator gives a few examples to start the process.

Ask the small groups to write down their ideas on a flip chart and feed back to the whole group.

Introduce the notion that self-esteem can be strongly affected by how people are treated and go through examples of actions to see if there were any other good or bad things that the group did not come up with.

Discuss the definition of self-esteem.

Question the group if they can think of anything else that may impact on how we view our self worth.

Agony aunt

Give out the 'Problem Page' activity sheet and ask participants to list the thoughts and feelings that the young person in the letter might be feeling and experiencing.

What could you do as a friend to help them feel better about their situation?

Trust game

Positive strokes

The facilitator sticks a sheet of A4 paper onto all the participants' backs and asks the participants to write something positive that they have noticed about other participants. Each participant should end up with a list of positive statements from each member of the group. Statements could include noticing how supportive they have been in the group, what good dress sense they have and so on.

Evaluation

Hand out evaluation sheets to each young person to fill in for the session. Encourage the young people to reflect on the session. Answer any questions participants may have about the group. Mention briefly what the contents of the following week's session will contain.

Activity Sheets for Session Three:

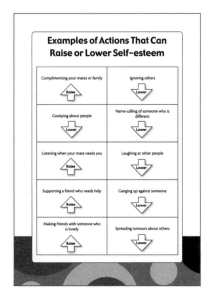

Examples of Actions That Can Raise or Lower Self-esteem

Complimenting your mates or family — **Raise**	Ignoring others — **Lower**
Gossiping about people — **Lower**	Name-calling of someone who is different — **Lower**
Listening when your mate needs you — **Raise**	Laughing at other people — **Lower**
Supporting a friend who needs help — **Raise**	Ganging up against someone — **Lower**
Making friends with someone who is lonely — **Raise**	Spreading rumours about others — **Lower**

Definitions of Self-esteem

'Feeling good about ourselves and in control of our lives.'

(Adams, 1997)

'Self-esteem refers to the extent to which we like and accept or approve of ourselves, how worthwhile a person we are.'

(Coopersmith, 1967, cited in Gross 1995)

'Self-esteem is really believing in your own worth and potential.'

(McCarthy, cited in Adams 1997)

'People who have positive self-esteem know that they are lovable and capable and they care about themselves and other people. They do not have to build themselves up by tearing other people down or by patronising less competent people.'

(Illsley-Clark, 1978, cited in Curry and Bromfield 1995)

Problem Page

Do you think this young person has low self-esteem?

Dear Problem Page

Please help. I have just moved into secondary school and there is a school trip coming up. I know I won't be able to go because my mum can't afford it. All the other girls in my class are talking about it and seem really excited about going away from home without their parents. I can't join in when they are all talking about what they will do and what they will take with them. I don't want to tell anyone about my situation because I don't want them to feel sorry for me. My new best mate at school keeps asking me about the trip and I just ignore her. I think she is getting fed up of me because she has started to hang around more with this other girl Sally. I don't even want to tell my mum about it because I know it will just stress her out more. She is on her own with me and my two brothers and she is stressed out enough trying to look after them. I try to help her as much as I can but it's hard. I already get called names and people laugh at me at school because of my clothes and shoes. I don't know what to do. I just keep making a mess of things.

Faye aged 11

Session Four

Assertiveness

Aim

For participants to understand the difference between aggressive, assertive, manipulative and passive.

For participants to practise assertive techniques, such as 'the broken record' and 'I statements'.

To help participants to feel more confident, more honest with themselves and others and more empowered to make decisions that acknowledge their own needs and feelings. For participants to become more aware of their own and other people's rights.

Overview

- ▶ Participants challenge negative thinking and try to turn them into positive statements.
- ▶ Explore participant's knowledge of what assertiveness means to them.
- ▶ Use role play to act out a scene and discuss different behaviours we may use to deal with the situation.
- ▶ To think about the techniques that may be useful to learn to help participants become more assertive.

Materials

- ▶ 'Challenge These Statements' activity sheet
- ▶ Flipchart paper and pens
- ▶ 'Role Play Scenario' activity sheet
- ▶ 'Assertive', 'Aggressive', 'Manipulative' and 'Passive' activity sheets
- ▶ 'Situation Cards' activity sheets
- ▶ 'Assertiveness Quiz' activity sheet
- ▶ 'Assertiveness Skills' activity sheet
- ▶ 'Body Language' activity sheet
- ▶ Evaluation sheets.

Check in

Welcome back to the group. Ask if participants have had any thoughts about the session from the week before.

Ice breaker

Challenging statements

Give out the 'Challenge These Statements' activity sheet and explain to the participants that they have to try to think of an alternative positive response to the statements on the sheet. Explain to participants that if we think negatively about a situation this can often lead us to feeling powerless and a spiral of negative thinking, but if we check out the validity of our thoughts and check the reality around us then we can often break the cycle of feeling negative. This allows us to problem-solve more easily and enables us to let go of issues that we have no control over. It is helpful if the facilitator demonstrates this process by giving participants a couple of examples.

What is assertiveness?

Start by asking the group to brainstorm what they think assertiveness means. Use a flip chart sheet to ask someone in the group to write down all the ideas participants come up with.

Assertiveness is a way of thinking and behaving that allows a person to stand up for his or her rights while respecting the rights of others. Non-assertive people may be passive or aggressive. Passive individuals are not committed to their own rights and are more likely to allow others to infringe on their rights than to stand up and speak out. On the other hand, aggressive people are more likely to defend their own rights and work to achieve their own goals but also likely to disregard the rights of others. Additionally, aggressive individuals insist that their feelings and needs take precedence over other people's. They also tend to blame others for problems instead of offering solutions.

A person with an assertive attitude recognises that each individual has rights. These rights include not only legal rights but also rights to individuality, to have and express personal preferences, feelings and opinions. The assertive individual not only believes in his or her rights but also is committed to preserving those rights. An assertive attitude is important in recognising that rights are being violated. The passive person is so concerned with being liked and accepted that he or she may never recognise the need to advocate. The assertive person clearly expresses his or her rights or needs. They tend to face problems promptly and they focus on solutions rather than problems.

Role play

Ask for two volunteers. One person is to be a store detective and the other to be a young person shopping. Read out the 'Role Play Scenario' sheet and ask the volunteers to act out the scene until the script reads stop.

At this point ask the rest of the participants to make suggestions about what should happen next. Ask the volunteers to act out the suggestions. Discuss with the group the differing responses.

It may be necessary for the group leaders to first participate in the role play in order to build up the confidence of the young people to take part.

Situation Cards

Give out 'Situation Cards' activity sheets that detail of examples of different behaviours and discuss the different types of behaviour. Split the participants into pairs and give each of them a Situation Card.

Ask the participants to practise the situation they have been given in a way that is passive, manipulative, aggressive and assertive.

Use the examples below to reinforce the different types of behaviour and to help the participants to demonstrate there given behaviour.

Manipulative

Jay asks her parents for money. She whines about it all day, tells them that all her friends get more than she does and says that she will feel left out if she can't buy what she wants. After a day of this, her parents reluctantly give in.

Aggressive

Sue asks for a lager in the bar. The barman refuses her because he thinks she is under age. Sue shouts and tells the barman to get stuffed, so he has her and her friends thrown out.

Assertive

Gill wants to borrow a new CD from Sharon. Sharon refuses so Gill asks if she can have it next week instead. Sharon says, 'OK.'

Passive

Barbara has very loud neighbours who play music late in the night. One night, past midnight, Barbara cannot sleep because of the noise. She goes round to the neighbours and asks them to turn the music down but they refuse and laugh at her. Barbara goes away feeling as though she has made a fool of herself by complaining.

Bring the group back together and discuss their responses and feelings about how they reacted.

Assertiveness Quiz (from www.headinjury.com/assertquiz.htm)

The facilitator gives out the assertiveness quiz to the participants and asks them to complete it individually. The facilitator then goes through the assertive answers and asks participants to note the answers on their sheet. The facilitator then explains why these are assertive responses.

Assertive Answers

1. No   2. Yes   3. No   4. Yes   5. No

6. No   7. Yes   8. No   9. Yes   10. No

Explanation of answers to the Assertiveness Quiz

1. The assertive person is not afraid to say no. She or he feels free to make choices.

2. The assertive person takes responsibility for getting his or her needs met. Fear of seeming ignorant does not prevent the assertive person from asking questions.

3. The assertive person takes responsibility for his or her own behaviour but does not take responsibility for the behaviour of others or for situations, which are beyond his or her control. To feel responsible for things beyond your control leads to unnecessary feelings of guilt.

4. Direct eye contact is assertive and suggests sincerity, self-confidence and the expectation that others will listen.

5. An assertive person wants to be heard.

6. An assertive person does not allow status to intimidate him or her.

7. Good posture communicates a positive self-image. When posture is limited by a disability, good eye contact and facial expression can be used to express a positive self-image.

8. The assertive person works to get his or her needs met and does not let situations build to the point of crisis.

9. The assertive person is able to ask for help without feeling dependent because he or she maintains a strong sense of self worth and self-respect.

10. Telling someone off is an angry, aggressive response. The assertive person would state that he or she is irritated by the unfairness and ask the person to move to the end of the line.

(Permission to use this quiz has been requested.)

Assertive techniques

Ask the young people to work back in pairs and with the same situation practise a particular assertive technique.

For example:

- ▸ 'Broken record', in which the young person repeatedly states what he needs from the situation with a calm voice.

- ▸ 'I statements', in which the young person ensures that when she is dealing with the situation that she does not generalise her remarks but owns them by stating, 'I want/need,' etc.

- Saying what you mean, being polite but straightforward. It is OK to say what you want.

- Saying NO. We find it difficult to say no because we don't want to be a spoilsport or be seen as mean, uncaring or unhelpful. We don't want to fall out with people so we may end up doing things we would rather not do. It is OK to say NO.

- Asking for more time before you make a decision, for example, Dawn asks, 'Can I borrow your bike tomorrow?' Colette replies, 'I might be using it but I'll have a think and ring you later.'

Give out the 'Assertiveness Skills' and the 'Body Language' activity sheets to all participants.

Evaluation

Hand out evaluation forms to each young person to fill in for the session. Encourage the young people to reflect on the session. Answer any questions participants may have about the group. Mention briefly what the contents of the following week's session will contain.

Activity Sheets for Session Four:

Challenge These Statements

People must love me or I will be miserable	
Making mistakes is terrible	
My emotions can't be controlled	
It is too difficult to be self-disciplined	
I can't stand the way others act	
Every problem has a perfect solution	
I can't change what I think	
If others pay attention to me I must have done something wrong	
I must never show any weakness	
Healthy people don't get upset	
People shouldn't act the way they do	
You can't tell me anything about me that I don't know	
I should be happy all the time	
It is others' responsibility to solve my problems	

Challenge These Statements
(some possible answers)

People must love me or I will be miserable.	I am responsible for my own happiness.
Making mistakes is terrible.	I learn from my mistakes.
My emotions can't be controlled.	I can decide how to respond if I feel something strongly.
It is too difficult to be self-disciplined.	I can learn skills to be self-disciplined if I choose to.
I can't stand the way others act.	Others actions are their responsibility. If I don't like the way someone is acting I can remove myself.
Every problem has a perfect solution.	There are no perfect solutions just solutions which might work.
I can't change what I think.	I have control over my own thoughts.
If others pay attention to me I must have done something wrong.	People pay attention to others for all sorts of reasons both good and bad.
I must never show any weakness.	Being open about my feelings and asking for support when I need it means I am more likely to get it.
Healthy people don't get upset.	Healthy people have a range of emotions that they are not afraid to show.
People ought to do what I wish.	I can ask people to help me but they have the right to refuse.
You can't tell me anything about me that I don't know.	I learn a lot about myself through my interactions with others.
I should be happy all the time.	I will take the opportunity to be happy as much as possible but I am aware that sometimes life is distressing.
It is others' responsibility to solve my problems.	I am responsible for my own wellbeing but this does not mean that I cannot ask for help.

What Is Assertiveness?

- Feeling confident
- Having self esteem
- Being myself
- Expressing myself
- Standing up for myself
- Feeling in control of my life
- Liking myself
- Respecting others and myself
- Making my own decisions
- Having the right to say yes and no for myself.

Role Play Scenario

The store detective stops the young person in the store because she believes that she is responsible for shoplifting. The young person is not responsible – they have stopped her because she looks like another young person whom a shop assistant had seen taking goods without paying for them. The young person is in a rush because she has to meet her friend.

Ask the volunteers to act out this initial scene.

STOP

Ask the young person what it felt like to be stopped and accused of something she had not done.

Ask the young person to try and explain how she feels, what kinds of emotions, fear, upset, anger, frustration etc. and also what is happening to her physically. Has her heart started to beat faster, are her hands sweating?

Ask the other participants what other feelings might be happening for the young person.

Now ask the store detective how she felt. How did the young person respond to her approach?

Did this make a difference to how she then wanted to carry on handling the situation?

Ask the group about what they thought about how the young person behaved?

Can they offer any different ways that the young person could have dealt with the situation?

Ask the young person offering the different solution to act out this with the store detective.

Discuss with the group whether there were any differences in the outcome from behaving in a different manner.

Which behaviours/actions led to better outcomes for the young person?

If the young person acted aggressively at first, ask the participants if they thought this helped the situation.

Discuss with the group that the person who has the power will always be the store detective and so if the young person responds aggressively she will never win the situation.

Ask the group what else you could do to get what you want and win the situation where you still feel okay about yourself.

Aggressive Behaviour

Aggressive Agnes

Out to win, Agnes puts people down. She is pushy and goes too far. She forces others to do things and does not listen to other people's point of view. She can be cruel and rude. She is bossy, wanting to take over and change others and always have the last word. She is very argumentative. She can be arrogant, always thinking she knows more than anyone else and can overreact and gets angry or explodes if she does not get her own way.

Passive Behaviour

Deana Doormat

Gives up, sits out, moans a lot and puts herself down. Helpless, saying, 'Why does it always happen to me?' Deana keeps quiet and never complains. She hates herself, gives herself a hard time. She tries to please other people, to make sure she's liked. She says sorry all the time, and she's never herself.

Indirect Behaviour

Manipulative Marie

Marie's indirect behaviour is dropping hints instead of saying something directly or asking for what she wants. Marie can also be cunning and sulks if she doesn't get her own way. She is sarcastic and rude, putting others down. She controls others and tries to make others feel guilty if they don't want what she wants. Marie goes 'round the houses' to ask for something. She denies her feelings and wriggles away leaving others feeling confused.

I really hate Susie, she always gets her own way. Just because she got a good mark in class she thinks she's it.

Assertive Behaviour

Assertive Andrea

Andrea is direct, honest, respects others, and is sincere. She is responsible for herself and asks for what she wants. She gets on with things and does not need others' approval. Andrea will take risks, doing new things and confronting her fears. She respects differences and listens to other people's points of view. She accepts both her positive and negative sides. She has a sense of her own worth and high self-esteem – she believes in herself.

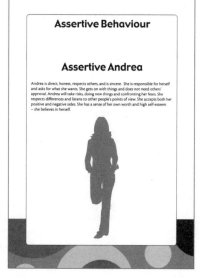

Assertiveness Quiz
(from www.headinjury.com/assertquiz.htm)
Permission requested

1. Do you buy things you do not want because you are afraid to say no to the salesperson?   Yes ☐ No ☐
2. When you do not understand the meaning of a word, do you ask about it?   Yes ☐ No ☐
3. Do you feel responsible when things go wrong, even if it is not your fault?   Yes ☐ No ☐
4. Do you look directly at others when you talk to them?   Yes ☐ No ☐
5. Do people often ask you to speak more loudly in order to be heard?   Yes ☐ No ☐
6. Do you feel intimidated by people in authority?   Yes ☐ No ☐
7. Do you generally have good posture?   Yes ☐ No ☐
8. Do you often feel so angry you could scream?   Yes ☐ No ☐
9. Do you know how to ask for help without feeling dependent?   Yes ☐ No ☐
10. If someone cuts in front of you in a line, do you usually tell them off?   Yes ☐ No ☐

Activity Sheets for Session Four continued:

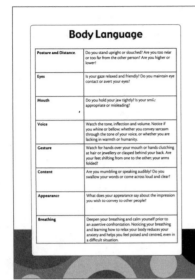

Body Language

Posture and Distance.	Do you stand upright or slouched? Are you too near or too far from the other person? Are you higher or lower?
Eyes	Is your gaze relaxed and friendly? Do you maintain eye contact or avert your eyes?
Mouth	Do you hold your jaw tightly? Is your smile appropriate or misleading?
Voice	Watch the tone, inflection and volume. Notice if you whine or bellow: whether you convey sarcasm through the tone of your voice, or whether you are lacking in warmth or humanity.
Gesture	Watch for hands over your mouth or hands clutching at hair or jewellery or clasped behind your back. Are your feet shifting from one to the other; your arms folded?
Content	Are you mumbling or speaking audibly? Do you swallow your words or come across loud and clear?
Appearance	What does your appearance say about the impression you wish to convey to other people?
Breathing	Deepen your breathing and calm yourself prior to an assertive confrontation. Noticing your breathing and learning how to relax your body reduces your anxiety and helps you feel poised and centred, even in a difficult situation.

Assertiveness Skills

1. BE SPECIFIC.

Decide what it is you want or feel and say so specifically and directly. Be clear. Be brief.

2. REPETITION.

This skill helps you to stay with your statement or request by using a calm repetition, over and over again.

3. FIELDING THE RESPONSE.

Indicate that you have heard what the other person says, so that you do not get 'hooked' by what they say. This skill helps you to acknowledge what the other person has said and still continue confidently with your statement.

4. WORKABLE COMPROMISE.

When your needs are in conflict with the needs and wishes of someone else, it is important to find a true compromise which considers you both.

1. Remember you have the right to make your wants known to others.

2. When you do not ask for what you want, you deny your own importance.

The best chance you have of getting exactly what you want is by asking for it specifically and directly. If you ask indirectly or drop hints, you run the risk of not being heard or understood and your request may go unheeded as a consequence.

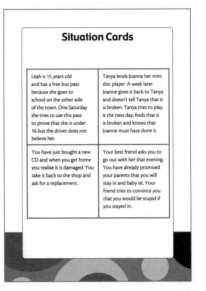

Situation Cards

Leah is 15 years old and has a free bus pass because she goes to school on the other side of the town. One Saturday she tries to use this pass to prove that she is under 16 but the driver does not believe her.	Tanya lends Joanne her mini disc player. A week later Joanne gives it back to Tanya and doesn't tell Tanya that it is broken. Tanya tries to play it the next day, finds that it is broken and knows that Joanne must have done it.
You have just bought a new CD and when you get home you realise it is damaged. You take it back to the shop and ask for a replacement.	Your best friend asks you to go out with her that evening. You have already promised your parents that you will stay in and baby sit. Your friend tries to convince you that you would be stupid if you stayed in.

Resources for Learning Mentors

Session Five

Stress and Relaxation

Aim

To examine what causes us stress and to recognise the general components of stress.

Overview

- ▸ An introduction to relaxation skills.
- ▸ An introduction to what causes us stress and what stress is.
- ▸ To begin to develop an awareness of the impact of stress on our thoughts, feelings, (emotional and physical) and on our behaviour.
- ▸ To develop ideas of effective coping strategies to deal with stress.

Materials

- ▸ 'Stilling Script' activity sheet
- ▸ Image of scales
- ▸ Scales
- ▸ Chocolate money or sweets
- ▸ Post-its
- ▸ Pens
- ▸ 'Scenario' activity sheets
- ▸ Large drawn outline of body
- ▸ 'Tips for Beating Stress' activity sheet
- ▸ Relaxation Scripts activity sheets
- ▸ Relaxation music
- ▸ 'Physical Symptoms of Stress' activity sheet
- ▸ Evaluation sheets.

Check in

Welcome back to the group. Ask if participants have had any thoughts about the session from the week before.

Ice breaker

Stilling

Inform participants that you are going to start with a quick relaxation technique called 'stilling'. Explain to them that this technique can help you to feel calm inside. It is useful to help you relax and concentrate at the same time.

It involves you sitting in the right position upright with your back against the chair and your feet flat on the floor.

It involves paying attention to your breathing.

Stilling is about letting go of what has been happening and focussing on the here and now.

Ask participants to sit comfortably in their chairs and read through the script.

What is stress?

Ask participants what causes them stress and ask them to write one idea each on post-its.

Ask them to stick the post-its on the scale drawing and place chocolate money/sweets in the real scales for each idea.

Explain that stress is a natural reaction to lots and lots of demands and pressure. It is not an illness. But if there is a lot of stress or if it goes on for a long time it can lead to problems with your health.

Stress is the way our bodies react to change.

These feelings can come from situations or people and can be good or bad.

Most people see stress as worry, tension and pressure but not all stress is bad.

We need stress in our lives or life would be dull.

They way we think and feel about a situation can make stress good or bad. For example, if you are moving house and were happy and excited about this, this would be a good stress, but if we are anxious and scared about moving then this would have a negative impact.

The demands placed on you have to be greater than your resources to cope with these demands for stress to have negative impact.

Stress indicators

Divide the participants into three groups with different coloured post-its for each group. Show the participants the 'Scenarios' activity sheets of a young person in a stressful situation.

One group writes down examples of thoughts or feelings experienced during stressful events (one per post-it), for example, anger.

The next group writes down physical sensations experienced during a stressful situation, for example, sweaty palms.

The final group writes down different behaviours associated with stress, for example, hitting somebody.

The participants are then encouraged to place the post-its on the body where they think that the feelings, sensations and behaviours are located.

Discussion about the placing of the post-its and the ideas generated is encouraged amongst the participants.

Dealing with stress

Bring participants back to the scales and ask them to write on post-its all the ways that they can deal with stress positively.

Place the post-its on the image of the scales and the chocolate money/sweets in the real scales. The challenge is to balance the scales out.

This demonstrates that we cannot always avoid stress but we can do things that counter balance the impact of stress.

Give out the 'Tips to Beat Stress' activity sheet.

Relaxation

When we are stressed, the muscles in our bodies tense up and this muscular tension causes uncomfortable feelings in the body, such as headache, backache, tight chest and so on.

These aches and pains of tension can cause mental worry, making us even more anxious and tense.

People who are tense often feel tired.

Relaxing slows down the systems in the body that speed up when we get anxious.

If we can learn to turn on the bodily symptoms of relaxation, we can turn off the symptoms of tension. They are two sides of the same coin: you can't experience feelings of relaxation and tension at the same time.

Ask participants to find a space on the floor and lay down on their backs without touching anyone else. Put on the relaxation music and read through a guided visualisation activity sheet (Guided Fantasy - Beach/Cloud, Magic Carpet, General Relaxation, Going On A Trip) or 'General Muscle Relaxation' activity sheet.

Evaluation

Hand out evaluation sheets to each young person to fill in for the session. Encourage the young people to reflect on the session. Answer any questions participants may have about the group. Mention briefly what the contents of the following week's session will contain

Activity Sheets for Session Five:

Stilling Script

Practise sitting comfortably in your chair making sure your back is straight and your head is facing the front. Relax your shoulders and rest your hands on your thighs, now let your eyes close gently... again make sure they are relaxed with the lids softly closed over them... Notice how quiet it is inside you... You are a still and quiet person inside you... If there are sounds outside of you besides my voice just notice them and let them go... Be relaxed, from your feet to the top of your head.

Now notice your breathing... notice the air passes into your nose, cool on the in-breath, warm on the out-breath... Count a few breaths, every out breath, 1 to 5... then start again... You are strong and peaceful... Now gently bring yourself back, stretching a little, taking some deep breaths... now look around slowly and come right back into the room, ready for what comes next.

Body

Physical Symptoms of Stress

Muscles tense up, ready for action. Your neck and shoulder muscles can feel tense and sore and can make your neck and back ache

Your brain sends a message, which gets more adrenaline in your body. This can make you headachy or dizzy. Your mind becomes more alert or can become confused.

Blood-clotting ability increases preparing for possible injury.

Your pupils widen. This can make your eyesight feel wobbly.

Nostrils and air passages in lungs open wider to get more air in quickly

Heartbeat speeds up. Blood pressure rises. Blood goes faster around your body. Sweating increases to help cool the body. Your blood comes up near the surface of the skin. This means you can go red/blush more and sweat more.

Blood is diverted to the muscles and you can look 'pale with fright'.

Immune responses decrease. Helpful in the short term to allow massive response to immediate threat. Harmful over a long period.

Liver releases sugar to provide quick energy. This can make your tummy feel unsettled and wobbly. Your tummy also slows down because the blood goes to other parts to help them when you are worried

The muscles around your bowels and bladder (sphincter muscles) relax, making you want to go to the toilet more often. They also contract to close openings of bowels and bladder.

Scenario 1

Scenario 2

Scenario 3

Tips to Beat Stress
(from: www.childstress.com)

Beating stress in your Body
- Have a bath
- Jump up and down 20 times
- Play football or do some other sport
- Avoid caffeine, it will make you feel more anxious
- Bash a pillow
- Put some music on and dance
- Ask for a cuddle
- Relax.

Beating stress in your Emotions
- Tell someone how you feel
- Write it down
- Draw how you feel
- Watch a happy video
- Go and talk to your pet
- Phone a friend.

Beating stress in your Actions
- Make something
- Help mum or dad
- Go outside and shout
- Wash someone's car
- Make a den in your room
- Hug someone or something
- Take some deep breaths
- Relax.

Beating stress in your Thoughts
- Write a story about it
- Read a book
- Tape record your thoughts
- Do a tricky puzzle
- Make a plan
- Think about things that have made you happy
- Think about all the things that you are good at.

Scales

Activity Sheets for Session Five Continued:

Guided Fantasy – Beach/Cloud

Sitting or lying comfortably, close your eyes.

Begin with calm breathing exercises.

Imagine yourself sitting on a towel on a beach. The sun is warm on your body and as you look around there is no one about. It's very quiet apart from the sound of a passing seagull. In your mind, you slowly stand up, you are barefoot, the warm sand runs freely between your toes. You look up at the sky, it is a deep blue with a few cotton wool ball clouds on the horizon. You breathe in the warm air.

You walk slowly down to the waters edge, the sea is gently lapping the shoreline, you walk into the clear blue water until it is gently splashing around your ankles. It feels cool and refreshing, you start to walk along the edge of the water, the wet sand is soft and your feet gently sink into it as you walk, you look round and see your footprints in the sand melting away into the sea.

You choose a warm area of sand and slowly sit down with your feet still in the water, you look out to sea and a boat is in the distance. As you watch it you see an odd white fluffy cloud in the sky, you watch it floating nearer. As it reaches above where you are sitting it gently gets lower until it is at the side of you.

You slowly stand and climb into the cloud, you feel how comfortable it is, you lay back and the cloud gently supports and caresses you. The cloud starts to float gently up into the sky, as you look down you can see the beach, the sea, the boat, it's warm and peaceful as you float along. You look at the world below as you gently float along, you feel calm and contented and just lay for a while feeling a gentle breeze on your cheeks and through your hair. Let yourself completely unwind as you relax breathing in the warm air.

After a while the cloud slowly and gently floats back down to where you were sat, you slowly sit up then stand and climb off the cloud. You stand with your feet at the water's edge and watch the cloud gently float back up into the sky. You walk slowly back along the beach to where your towel is and you slowly sit down.

Now bring yourself back into this room and slowly open your eyes and begin to think about the movements you will make to sit up. When you are ready, sit up and move around to make yourself more comfortable.

Guided Fantasy – Magic Carpet

Sitting or lying comfortably, close your eyes.

Begin with calm breathing exercises.

Imagine yourself walking out of this building and seeing a magic carpet outside. You get on to the carpet and make yourself comfortable. You are going to fly right away from here to somewhere much warmer. You are flying above towns and villages, field and farms. The houses and cars look unreal, like matchbox toys. Now you are over a beach and now the sea. At first the sea is grey but as we get to a warmer climate it gets bluer and bluer. You can feel the sun beating down on you.

Ahead you see a lush island with palm trees, white sand and clear blue sea. You land on the beach and look around for a minute or two breathing in the richly scented warm air. You take a stroll on the beach barefooted and feel the warmth of the sand on the soles of your feet. Dip your toes in the sea, it feels warm but refreshing.

Now walk into the jungle. There are beautiful exotic flowers everywhere - they smell wonderful and are clear bright colours - pinks, yellow, turquoise. High above you there are monkeys jumping from tree to tree chattering to each other and parrots flying around. Ahead you see a clearing in the jungle and walk towards it. There is a sleepy green lagoon bathed in green light from the sun passing through the tallest palm trees. On the lagoon is a little dinghy and you get into it and lie down.

You are bobbing gently in the lagoon in a pool of green light. You can hear the monkeys and birds screeching in the jungle but they sound a long way away.

You can smell the musky fragrance of the exotic flowers and fruit on the trees. Just enough sun can get through the trees to warm your body as you lie on the dinghy. Let yourself completely unwind as you relax breathing in the warmth and smells, hearing the sounds of the jungle.

When you are ready to come back, get up from the dinghy, walk slowly back through the jungle to your magic carpet. Make yourself comfortable on the carpet again ready for the journey home. You are flying back over the sea, then over land and now you can see your hometown. You land back where you started from and walk back into the room.

General Relaxation

This is a relaxation procedure that focuses on your muscles and how they feel. It uses the building up and letting go of muscle tension to help you learn to relax.

First of all you need to make yourself as comfortable as you can.

Take your time to do this now.

Ten seconds of silence.

As you sit or lie become aware of the sensations of the room around you. Notice any sounds you can hear. Notice the temperature of the air in your room and the feeling of your clothes. Just explore those sensations and become aware of them as you can and just enjoy any that feel particularly pleasant.

Ten seconds of silence.

To help you relax it is good to focus on simple sensations.

Ten seconds of silence

And now I would like you to focus on the feelings in your muscles. Just become aware of how your muscles are feeling. Either loose or tight, relaxed or tense or whatever. Just become aware of how they are feeling now.

20 seconds of silence.

And then I would like you to focus more on the muscles in your tummy. Become aware on how your tummy muscles are feeling. Just notice how you are holding those muscles.

Five seconds of silence.

And now I would like you to tense those muscles as much as you are able to.

Three seconds of silence.

Just notice how it feels to have them tense and hold them for a moment...

And now let go of the tension let the muscles relax. Notice how it feels to let go. Really notice the difference between the muscles being relaxed and them being tense.

Five seconds of silence.

Progressive Muscle Relaxation

Sit or lie down in a comfortable position. Relax yourself to the best of your ability.

Consider the various muscle groups one at a time, and aim to learn the difference between tight and relaxed muscles. Try constantly to concentrate on the feeling in the muscle as it goes from tight to loose.

Hands and arms.

Clench your fists, and tense your arms; feel tightness in your hands and arms, then slowly relax them.

See how far they will go, but do not push.

Do not hold on at all; let everything go.

Shoulders

Hunch your shoulders, then gradually let them settle down.

See how far they will go, but do not push.

Do not hold on at all; let everything go.

Forehead

Pull your eyebrows together, then gradually let your forehead smooth out.

Do not hold on at all; let everything go.

Eyes

Screw your eyes up tight, then gradually let them smooth out, leaving your eyes closed, feeling your eyeballs sink, and your eyelids droop.

Let them get really heavy.

Jaw

Bite your back teeth together, then gradually ease off, and let your jaw get heavy.

Back of neck

Pull your chin forward on to your chest, feel tightness, then relax.

Going On A Trip

Find a space and either sit upright or lay down on your back.

Today we are going to use our imaginations, that part of the mind that sees pictures and creates anything we wish. Before we start, slowly and quietly take some deep breaths. Inhale, hold the breath for a moment, then slowly release it. Feel your body becoming relaxed and comfortable, the floor supporting you. And as your body becomes still, your mind becomes open and alert.

Now I would ask you to let your imagination take you to a small island. It's got fields, trees, streams, a river, a beach and the sea. It's a lovely place, somewhere you like to be. The sun is shining and warm, the wind is blowing gently, the birds are singing.

You can decide just where you want to go, do what you want to do. Think of one thing you would like to do, walk in the woods, climb to the top of a tree, sit in a field, lie on the beach, paddle in the sea. You decide and then do it (pause).

Really enjoy doing it. Feel the grass or the sand or the water, whatever it is.

Do what you like without hurrying, no one is going to tell you to do something different. Is there anything to hear where you are?... anything to smell?... anything to touch? What is the best thing about where you are on your island? This is a special place you have found. Really enjoy being there and realise how wonderful it is (pause).

Remember this is a place you can return to at any time. Now, in your own time, when you are ready, I would like you to come back to the room.

Have a slow stretch, open your eyes, sit up and return to wherever you are.

Programme 3

Session Six

Hopes, Fears and Dreams

Aim

To explore individual aspirations and hopes for the future. To consider their realistic options and to look at what they will need to start doing in order to achieve their goals.

Overview

- ▸ To consider our hopes and fears when thinking about the future.

- ▸ Participants run through exercises that help them plan for the future, using a future lifeline to explore their options.

Materials

- ▸ 'Future Lifeline' activity sheet

- ▸ Option Cards

- ▸ Flip chart paper/pens

- ▸ Ball of string or wool

- ▸ Scissors

- ▸ Evaluation sheets.

Check in

Welcome back to the group. Give participants time to raise any issues they have from last week's session.

Ice breaker

My crystal ball

Ask each participant to predict the future of the other group members. Give each participant a piece of A4 paper so that they can write down their predictions. Ask them to consider their fellow group members when they are 30 and think about:

- ▸ what career will they have?

- ▸ what kind of house will they live in?

- ▸ where will they live?

- ▸ will they have any children?

Or play the following game as an alternative.

The best thing that happened to me this week

In a round each participant finishes off the statement:

'The best thing that happened to me this week was...'

It can be followed by different rounds such as:

'If I had this week to live over what I would change is...'

'If I was a famous person I would be...'

'I'd like to write a book about...'

'If I were an animal I would be a...' '

'Some things I want to do before I die are...' and so on.

Hopes, Fears and Dreams

On a flipchart write 'Hopes', 'Fears' and 'Dreams' and ask the participants to brainstorm their own hopes, fears and dreams for the future.

Participants share with the group some of their ideas. Discuss any issues that arise, e.g. difficulty of looking into the future if you do not know where you are going to be living in the next few months.

Future lifeline

Give out the 'Future Lifeline' activity sheet and Option Cards. Ask participants to fill in the lifeline individually.

Help the participants think about where they would like to be heading: career, college, being a parent etc. Participants share some of their options with the group and, if there are gaps in the lifeline, discuss what the blocks may be to making decisions, for example, is it too far ahead to think about?

Ask participants to brainstorm things that help achieve goals and write them on flipchart, e.g. personal skills, Connexions, research on the internet, attending careers fairs, support from family, and determination.

Trust game

Saying goodbye

Participants sit in a circle with one member holding a ball of string or wool.

The participant with the ball looks around and says a goodbye and a final message to one of the other participants. Holding on to the end of the string/wool they throw the ball to the participant they said the goodbye to.

The person who receives the ball then repeats the process.

This carries on until the process comes to a natural end.

At the end there is silence and the facilitator then cuts all the string that is now criss-crossing the circle, symbolising the end of the group.

Evaluation

Hand out evaluation sheets to each young person to fill in for the session. Encourage the young people to reflect on the session and the groupwork programme as a whole. Hand out certificates of completion.

Activity Sheets for Session Six:

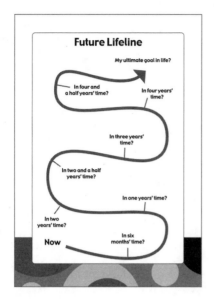

Programme 4

Healthy Minds Workshop

A course to promote mental health and wellbeing

Thank you to Jane Sedgewick, Zoe Brownlie, Trish Smith-O'Shea and Gill Crow for their ideas, which contributed to this workshop

Contents

Foreword by Mark Heaton

Introduction

Activity One: What is Mental Health?

Activity Two: Mind and Body Exercise

Activity Three: Continuum Line and Coping Cards

Activity Four: Relaxation Resources

On the CD-ROM

○ Evaluation Sheet

○ Physical Symptoms of Stress

○ Body

○ 3 x Scenarios

○ Credit Cards

○ Going On A Trip

○ Guided Fantasy: Beach/Cloud

○ Guided Fantasy: Magic Carpet

○ General Relaxation

○ Progressive Muscle Relaxation

○ Certificate

Foreword

Government policies in education increasingly recognise that social, emotional and behavioural skills (SEBS) underlie almost every aspect of school, home and community life. These include:

- being effective and successful learners
- improving academic performance
- making and sustaining friendships
- dealing with and resolving conflict
- managing strong feelings such as frustration, anger and anxiety
- promoting calm and optimistic states that promote the achievement our goals
- recovering from setbacks and persisting in the face of difficulties
- working (and playing) cooperatively
- recognising and standing up for their rights and those of others
- understanding and valuing the commonalities and differences between people
- respecting the right to have beliefs and values that are different to our own.

This has played an important role in the development of several key policy areas, which should have far reaching benefits for young people.

The Public Health White Paper *Choosing Health* (DH, 2004) set out the Government's intention for all schools to become 'Healthy Schools'. *Every Child Matters*, and the subsequent Children Act of 2004, sets out five national outcomes for children. Healthy Schools can make a significant contribution towards achieving these outcomes. DfES and DH fund the programme jointly. The aim is for every child, whatever their background or their circumstances, to have the support they need to:

- be healthy
- stay safe
- enjoy and achieve
- make a positive contribution
- achieve economic wellbeing.

The outcomes are mutually reinforcing. For example, children and young people learn and thrive when they are healthy, safe and engaged, and the evidence shows clearly that educational achievement is the most effective route out of poverty.

One of the aims of the Healthy Schools Programme is to promote positive emotional health and wellbeing by helping pupils to understand and express their feelings, build their confidence and emotional resilience and therefore their capacity to learn. Support systems should be in place for pupils and staff to access advice to manage major life changes, with explicit values underpinning positive emotional health. It is also vital that the school provides on-going opportunities for pupils to develop healthy levels of self-esteem.

Achieving National Healthy School status enables schools to demonstrate its contribution to the five national outcomes for children and supports the targets within other national priorities around improving behaviour and attendance, including the Secondary Strategy's Social, Emotional and Behavioural Skills (SEBS) Pilot. This programme is based on evidence in 2005 that, 'shows that these skills are central to personal and professional success in life' (The Tomlinson Report, the Steer Report and Ofsted Report).

These skills are also the basis for the Social and Emotional Aspects of Learning (SEAL), which is a key element in the Primary National Strategy. The SEAL resource provides a framework for explicitly promoting SEBS, with built-in progression for each year group within a school. The resource aims to provide schools and settings with an explicit, structured whole-curriculum framework for developing all children's SEBS.

Evidence shows the importance of a sound education in promoting better health and emotional wellbeing for all children and young people and, in particular, those who are socially and economically disadvantaged (Independent Inquiry into Inequalities in Health, 1998). Schools are key settings in which to improve both physical and emotional health and educational achievement. With this in mind it is clear that the Healthy Minds Workshop can make a significant contribution to this, with a resource that is compatible with the ECM, Healthy Schools, SEAL and SEBS agendas.

Mark Heaton (Behaviour Consultant)

Quality Improvement and Support Service, CYPD, Sheffield City Council

Introduction

Mental health is not something that is generally talked about, which often results in a lack of understanding. Good mental health is much more than the absence of mental illness, it is about being self-aware and having self-respect. It is also about having the capacity to have some power, control and choice in your life.

The NHS Health Advisory Service defined mental health as:

- ▸ the ability to develop psychologically, emotionally, intellectually and spiritually

- ▸ the ability to initiate, develop and sustain mutually satisfying personal relationships

- ▸ the ability to become aware of others and empathise with them

- ▸ the ability to use psychological distress as a developmental process, so that it does not hinder or impair further development.

The charity Young Minds states:

...Mental health... refers to the capacity to live a full productive life as well as the flexibility to deal with its ups and downs. In children and young people it is especially about the capacity to learn, to enjoy friendships, to meet challenges, to develop talents and capabilities.

The terms 'mental health problems', 'mental health disorders' and 'mental illness' refer to different degrees of distress, confusion and disturbance that children and young people may experience.

Mental Health Problems affect an estimated 25% of children and young people at any one time. These problems interfere with children and young people's ability to learn, enjoy friendships and deal with adversity. Some children may be over anxious and frightened whilst others may be mistrustful and angry.

Mental Health Disorders affect 10% of the population of children and young people. These disorders are similar to 'problems' but are usually more severe, complex or persistent and need specialist help and treatment. Such disorders include emotional disorders and conduct (behavioural) disorders.

Mental Illness affects a very small proportion of children and young people. Psychosis, clinical depression and extreme forms of anorexia nervosa are some examples and often there is a biological basis to such difficulties.

Good mental health is the emotional and spiritual resilience, which enables us to enjoy life and to survive pain, disappointment and sadness. It is a positive sense of wellbeing and an underlying belief in our own, and other's, dignity and worth.

Mental health underpins all health and wellbeing. It influences how we think and feel about ourselves and others, how we interpret events, our capacity to learn, to communicate and to form and sustain relationships.

Mental health is influenced by many variables including individual coping skills and levels of social support, as well as structural factors like adequate housing, employment and financial security. Most people will experience life events that are stressful and can affect mental wellbeing, for example, the death of a partner, the birth of a child, redundancy, retirement or ill health. In addition some people suffer the chronic stress of coping with poverty, exclusion, unemployment and discrimination, which also undermines mental health.

Stress or mental distress can damage physical health. Although the exact way in which this happens is not fully understood, negative stress suppresses the body's immune system, reduces resilience to disease and also increases the risk of coronary heart disease.

Everyone has mental health needs and mental health promotion can benefit us all. Mental health promotion works to strengthen people's capacity for mental health, whether or not they currently have a mental health problem. It also has a role to play in working to reduce factors, which are known to damage mental wellbeing.

Mental health problems are common and can affect anyone. At any one time one in seven adults is experiencing a mental health problem, and in any one-year, the figures rise to one in four adults. (Mind, 2002). In spite of this, mental health issues are often deeply taboo and surrounded with fear and misunderstanding. The stigma attached to mental health problems adds greatly to the distress and isolation felt by people who have experienced problems and may also inhibit people from seeking help.

Introduction

In a large group:

- ▶ Introduce self and colleagues.

- ▶ Explain who you are and what you do (you are interested in how people think and feel about themselves and their lives and their health).

- ▶ Briefly mention how you are going to work. You will be working mostly in smaller groups. Each group will have an adult to help them and there isn't a lot of time so you all have to work quickly and concentrate.

- ▶ Explain to participants that you are now going to split them up into smaller groups by giving them a number (one, two or three) or apples, oranges or pears. They are now going to do a short activity in the smaller groups.

The activities work best with ten participants. If you only have a small group divide them accordingly. You can also run the activities as a whole group exercise. This means that some participants will not have the same level of support to join in and participate.

Activity One

What is Mental Health?

Aim

To explore young people's knowledge of mental health and discuss the myths and misconceptions young people might have about mental health. The session will focus on the term 'mental health' and compare it to the young people's views and attitudes to physical health.

Materials

Each group:

‣ Flip chart with 'mental health' written on a page

‣ Flip chart pen.

Method

The group should come up with as many words as possible that they associate with the term 'Mental Health' and a scribe in the group should write them on the flipchart paper provided.

The groups should then feed back to the whole group the words they came up with. The facilitator then pulls out common themes from the group and presents statistics about young people's mental wellbeing.

The facilitator asks a member of the group to volunteer to scribe, reminding or introducing the group to the principles of doing a brainstorm.

‣ Someone needs to volunteer as a 'scribe' or you nominate someone.

‣ Suggest things that come into your mind when you hear the term... (in this case 'Mental Health').

‣ Everyone's contributions are written down.

‣ No one to comment on what gets written down.

Purpose

To explain that we all have mental health and it is not just about illness. The facilitator ensures that the focus is turned around to look at positive aspects of mental health.

Conclusion and statistics

Ask the group to think about the words 'physical health' and to shout out any ideas that come into their mind when they think about this word. The facilitator then points out that it is interesting that often we think of illness when we talk about mental health but if we talked about physical health we would consider a whole range of things from being fit to terminal illness. Mental health is not just about severe illness but is to do with our emotional wellbeing, and problems with our mental health can range from mild to severe. Some statistics about young peoples' mental health problems include facts such as:

‣ 1 in 3 nine year old girls are worried about their weight and many are already dieting.

‣ About a third of girls and a quarter of boys 14-15 years old are sometimes afraid to go to school because of bullying (1995 figures).

‣ An estimated 25% of junior and middle school pupils are being bullied.

‣ BT estimates that 10,000 children try to call ChildLine every day.

- Of over 900 young people surveyed in Surrey in 1995, 33% said they had been so depressed that they wanted to harm themselves and 26% had actually considered suicide.

- Suicide is now the second most common cause of death for young men after road accidents.

- Suicide accounts for 20% of all deaths by young people.

- Around 19,000 young people are admitted to hospital for deliberate self-harm each year.

- 1 in 10 adolescents who have deliberately harmed themselves will do so on more than one occasion.

- 8 -11% of children and young people experience anxiety to such an extent that it affects their ability to get on with their everyday lives.

- 2% of children under the age of 12 have some form of depression, compared with 5% of teenagers.

- Hyperactivity is prevalent in children, but this varies according to the criteria used to measure hyperactivity. It is from 2-17% of boys aged between 5-11 years, depending on the criteria used.

- 1 in 4 children who live in inner cities will have significant mental health problems, compared with 1 in 10 in rural areas.

- Social deprivation such as poverty, unemployment and crime place children and young people at greater risk of developing mental health problems.

- Family divorce, bereavement of a parent and experience of neglect or abuse also places children and young people at greater risk.

- Risk is also increased if a child or young person has a health or development problem or has a family member with a mental health problem.

Activity Two

Mind and Body

Aim

To introduce to young people that stressful life events have an impact on our mental and physical health in a sequential order.

Materials

Each group:

- ▶ 'Body' activity sheet
- ▶ 'Scenario' activity sheets
- ▶ post-its in three different colours
- ▶ pens.

Method

The smaller groups are further split down into three groups each with a different colour post-it. The participants are asked to think about the young person in the picture and to come up with as many words as possible to describe how that young person may be; group one: thinking and feeling emotionally; group two: physically feeling and group three: how that young person may behave or act. The groups write their ideas onto the post-it notes, one idea per post-it. The small groups, in turn, then place post-its on to the 'Body' activity sheet where they think it is most appropriate.

Once the activity is complete handout the 'Physical Symptoms of Stress' activity sheet and 'Scenario' activity sheets from the CD-ROM and go through the physical symptoms that the participants may not have known about.

- ▶ Now in your groups we want you to look at the 'Scenario' sheet given to you. Putting yourself in the place of the young person in the picture, think about how our minds and bodies might react in such situations.

- ▶ The adult in your group will then split you up into three smaller groups and each group will concentrate on one of three aspects:

1. How the young person might feel and think emotionally (for example, scared, upset, angry, shocked).

2. How the young person might feel in their body or physically feel (for example, butterflies, dry mouth, shaking, sweaty).

3. How they might behave or act (for example, cry, runaway, hit out, take it out on someone or something else).

Purpose

To explore the connection between stressful situations and how both our minds and bodies are affected and inter related in a sequential order – thoughts, physical feelings and behaviour. The facilitator links the fact that when a stressful situation happens to us we all have a response that is emotional and physical and this influences our behaviour. The linking of the body to thoughts and circumstances helps people to learn about triggers that induce certain feelings.

Programme 4

Activity Sheets for Activity Two:

Physical Symptoms of Stress

Muscles tense up, ready for action. Your neck and shoulder muscles can feel tense and sore and can make your neck and back ache

Your brain sends a message, which gets more adrenaline in your body. This can make you headachy or dizzy. Your mind becomes alert or can become confused.

Blood-clotting ability increases preparing for possible injury.

Your pupils widen. This can make your eyesight feel wobbly.

Nostrils and air passages in lungs open wider to get more air in quickly

Heartbeat speeds up. Blood pressure rises. Blood goes faster around your body. Sweating increases to help cool the body. Your blood comes up near the surface of the skin. This means you can go red/blush more and sweat more.

Blood is diverted to the muscles and you can look 'pale with fright'.

Immune responses decrease. Helpful in the short term to allow massive response to immediate threat. Harmful over a long period.

Liver releases sugar to provide quick energy. This can make your tummy feel unsettled and wobbly. Your tummy also slows down because the blood goes to other parts to help them when you are worried.

The muscles around your bowels and bladder (sphincter muscles) relax, making you want to go to the toilet more often. They also contract to close openings of bowels and bladder.

Body

Scenario 1

Scenario 2

Scenario 3

Activity Three

Continuum Line and Coping Cards

Aim

To focus on the positive things we can do to help ourselves feel better in stressful situations and how we can give and receive support in order to maintain our emotional wellbeing or mental health. In order to achieve good mental health we need to have access to resources that increase our resilience to adversity. There are three fundamental building blocks that underpin resilience. A secure base, where young people feel a sense of belonging and security; good self-esteem, which is an internal sense of self-worth and competence and a sense of self-efficacy, which is a sense of mastery and control and an accurate understanding of personal strengths and limitations (Daniel, Wassell & Gilligan, 1999).

Materials

Each group:

- Pieces of A4 paper with '0', '5' and '10' written on them

- 'Scenario' activity sheets.

Method

Using the pictures from the mental health awareness session the facilitator explains to the group that there is a scale of 0-10, 0 being feeling very bad and 10 being feeling very good.

The facilitator places the A4 paper with 0, 5 and 10 onto the floor in a line. The facilitator then asks the participants to place themselves physically on the imaginary continuum line of where they believe the young person in the scene would be in relation to the way they might be feeling.

Once settled on the line, the facilitator asks the participants why they have placed themselves in that position. If participants have placed themselves near or on 0 the facilitator asks them what they would do to make themselves feel better to move them up the scale. If they have placed themselves near the top of the scale, the facilitator elicits what has helped the participant to stay feeling so well.

Some participants bring up the use of drugs or alcohol as a way to make them feel better. It is important as a facilitator that you explain that this is only a temporary solution and can lead to consequences that can further damage your mental wellbeing. It can lead to interesting debates if you ask the participants what they think some of the consequences to these actions may be.

It is also important to allow the young people themselves to decide how far they would move up the scale with the coping skill they have chosen, for example, talk to a friend.

- Still in your groups we would like to try and illustrate how events in people's lives can affect them and make them feel different. It is possible for people to feel bad about who they are and at other times feel good.

- Still thinking of the young person in the scenario and imaging we have a scale from 0 -10 we would like you to place yourself on this imaginary line in a position were you think the young person in the picture is likely to be in relation to the way they might be feeling.

- Once settled on the line, ask different individuals why they have placed themselves where they have. If they are near 0, try and elicit what might have to happen to move them up the scale. If they are near 10 ask them what has helped them stay feeling well. (Introducing the notion of healthy and unhealthy coping strategies).

- For example: if the young person places themselves at 0, ask them what they could do that might make them feel better about the situation. If they say talk to a friend, ask them how far up the scale that might put them. If they say fight back, ask them if there would be any adverse consequences to this behaviour.

Purpose

To elicit reasoning behind the young person placing themselves at various points on the scale and to begin to discuss coping strategies that would influence them moving up the scale towards 10.

To introduce the notion that mental wellbeing is not a static condition and that we all move up and down a scale of emotional wellness and that we all have mental health which is affected by life events and can be counteracted by individual coping strategies and supports available.

Facilitator's notes

Some positive steps that young people can take include:

1. Being aware of mental health issues and sources of help.

2. Looking after your own physical health - regular exercise, balanced diet and regular sleep.

3. Talking through problems with friends, family or teachers and being prepared to take action.

4. Being aware of your emotions and expressing your feelings.

5. Knowing how to relax - breathing exercises, relaxation techniques, massage and meditation.

6. Trying out new activities which challenge you - extending your comfort zone.

7. Learning from others and listening to their point of view.

8. Avoiding the use of alcohol, drugs or substances to cope with problems.

9. Participating more in school and community activities - feeling a part of things.

Contingency activity – Coping Cards

Aim

To allow young people the time to come up with three positive coping strategies that they think would work for them in stressful situations.

Materials

- ‣ 'Credit Cards' activity sheet

- ‣ Pens.

If you have a very quiet group and you are waiting for the other groups to finish before the relaxation session begins you can end the session on a positive note by asking the young people to think of their own personal coping strategies.

Method

The facilitator gives out the cards to the young people and asks them to write down three things they can do to help themselves when they are feeling stressed. This card is for the young people to take away with them and keep to remind themselves of the things they can do if they are feeling bad. It is important that the facilitator helps the young people to write down positive coping strategies and not unhealthy coping strategies.

- ‣ Hand out cards to the group and ask them to write down three things they can do for themselves that would be a healthy way of dealing with their own stress, anxiety or fears

- ‣ Ensure that the young people are writing down positive ways of coping. You may need to draw on some of the methods they suggested in the previous activity. But try to get the young people to come up with something that could work for them personally.

Purpose

To end the session on a positive note with the participants taking away their own individual ways of thinking and dealing with issues that may affect their emotional wellbeing. Often when we are stressed or distressed we find it very difficult to remember the kinds of things that can help us to feel better about our lives or ourselves. Writing things down is one way to help us remember. Having a handy sized card, which can be put somewhere accessible, is also helpful.

Activity Sheets for Activity Three:

Activity Four

Relaxation Session

Aim

To introduce a healthy coping strategy that can reduce the physical symptoms of stress.

Materials

- ▸ Relaxation script activity sheets
- ▸ Relaxation tape
- ▸ Cassette recorder
- ▸ Room that is large enough and comfortable enough for young people to lie down
- ▸ Evaluation sheets.

Method

The facilitator asks the small groups to come back to the large group to discuss some of the ideas they came up with regarding healthy ways of coping with stress. The facilitator then introduces the notion that relaxation is one technique that young people could learn to help them with all sorts of stressful situations such as exam stress. The participants are asked to find a space on the floor not touching anyone else and to lie on their backs with their legs flat. The relaxation music is put on and the facilitator reads a script of their choice.

Once the relaxation has finished the facilitator asks the participants how they found the exercise. Whether it was difficult to get your body to relax and to explain that it is a technique that needs practice for you to get the most benefit out of it. It can also help to inform young people that many people use relaxation techniques to help them to focus, such as sports people and actors.

- ▸ We are now going to demonstrate one way you can help yourself if you are feeling stressed. This is a healthy way to deal with problems or worries.

- ▸ We would like you to find a space on the floor and lie down on your back.

- ▸ If you feel really uncomfortable lying down then you can stay sat in your chair, but you must sit up straight with your feet firmly placed flat on the floor and your hands resting on your knees.

- ▸ Once you are comfortable we will start. (Put relaxation music on and begin). We would like you to close your eyes, everyone but myself will have their eyes closed.

Purpose

To give young people the experience of learning new ways of dealing with stress and to reinforce the fact that the physical symptoms of stress can be reduced by allowing our bodies to relax.

Relaxation

Why is relaxation helpful?

When we are stressed, the muscles in our bodies tense up and this muscular tension causes uncomfortable feelings in the body, such as headache, backache, tight chest and so on.

These aches and pains of tension can cause mental worry, making us even more anxious and tense.

People who are tense often feel tired.

Relaxing slows down the systems in the body that speed up when we get anxious.

If we can learn to turn on the bodily symptoms of relaxation, we can turn off the symptoms of tension. They are two sides of the same coin: you can't experience feelings of relaxation and tension at the same time.

Relaxation is a skill

The ability to relax is not always something that comes naturally, it is a skill that has to be learnt and practiced. The following exercises are designed to help you learn to relax. Some of the exercises are quite long to start with, but as you get used to them, you can begin to shorten the routines. This should be done gradually until you are able to relax at will, as you need to.

General guidelines

1. Try to decide in advance when you are going to practise; in this way you can develop a routine that you can stick to. Make time for yourself.

2. Make sure that you choose somewhere quiet to relax, and make sure that no one will disturb you during your practice.

3. Don't attempt your exercise if you are hungry or have just eaten, or if the room is too hot or chilly.

4. Try to adopt a 'passive' attitude, that is, do not worry about your performance or whether you are successful in relaxing. Just 'have a go' and let it happen.

Try to breathe through your nose, using your stomach muscles. Try to breathe slowly and regularly. It is important that you do not take a lot of quick, deep breaths as this can make you feel dizzy or faint and even make your tension worse. When you place your hands on your stomach, you will feel the movement if you are breathing properly. Try this out before you exercise, to make sure that you are used to the feeling.

After completing a relaxation, always get up slowly - you may feel dizzy or faint if you get up too quickly.

Activity Sheets for Activity Four:

Going On A Trip

Find a space and either sit upright or lay down on your back.

Today we are going to use our imaginations, that part of the mind that sees pictures and creates anything we wish. Before we start, slowly and quietly take some deep breaths. Inhale, hold the breath for a moment, then slowly release it. Feel your body becoming relaxed and comfortable, the floor supporting you. And as your body becomes still, your mind becomes open and alert.

Now I would ask you to let your imagination take you to a small island. It's got fields, trees, streams, a river, a beach and the sea. It's a lovely place, somewhere you like to be. The sun is shining and warm, the wind is blowing gently, the birds are singing.

You can decide just where you want to go, do what you want to do. Think of one thing you would like to do, walk in the woods, climb to the top of a tree, sit in a field, lie on the beach, paddle in the sea. You decide and then do it (pause).

Really enjoy doing it. Feel the grass or the sand or the water, whatever it is.

Do what you like without hurrying, no one is going to tell you to do something different. Is there anything to hear where you are?... anything to smell?... anything to touch? What is the best thing about being where you are on your island? This is a special place you have found. Really enjoy being there and realise how wonderful it is (pause).

Remember this is a place you can return to at any time. Now, in your own time, when you are ready, I would like you to come back to the room.

Have a slow stretch, open your eyes, sit up and return to wherever you are.

Guided Fantasy – Beach/Cloud

Sitting or lying comfortably, close your eyes.

Begin with calm breathing exercises.

Imagine yourself sitting on a towel on a beach. The sun is warm on your body and as you look around there is no one about. It's very quiet apart from the sound of a passing seagull. In your mind, you slowly stand up, you are barefoot, the warm sand runs freely between your toes. You look up at the sky, it is a deep blue with a few cotton wool ball clouds on the horizon. You breathe in the warm air.

You walk slowly down to the waters edge, the sea is gently lapping the shoreline, you walk into the clear blue water until it is gently splashing around your ankles. It feels cool and refreshing, you start to walk along the edge of the water, the wet sand is soft and your feet gently sink into it as you walk, you look round and see your footprints in the sand melting away into the sea.

You choose a warm area of sand and slowly sit down with your feet still in the water, you look out to sea and a boat is in the distance. As you watch it you see an odd white fluffy cloud in the sky, you watch it floating nearer. As it reaches above where you are sitting it gently gets lower until it is at the side of you.

You slowly stand and climb into the cloud, you feel how comfortable it is, you lay back and the cloud gently supports and caresses you. The cloud starts to float gently up into the sky, as you look down you can see the beach, the sea, the boat, it's warm and peaceful as you float along. You look at the world below as you gently float along, you feel calm and contented and just lay for a while feeling a gentle breeze on your cheeks and through your hair. Let yourself completely unwind as you relax breathing in the warm air.

After a while the cloud slowly and gently floats back down to where you were sat, you slowly sit up then stand and climb off the cloud. You stand with your feet at the water's edge and watch the cloud gently float back up into the sky. You walk slowly back along the beach to where your towel is and you slowly sit down.

Now bring yourself back into this room and slowly open your eyes and begin to think about the movements you will make to sit up. When you are ready, sit up and move around to make yourself more comfortable.

Guided Fantasy – Magic Carpet

Sitting or lying comfortably, close your eyes.

Begin with calm breathing exercises.

Imagine yourself walking out of this building and seeing a magic carpet outside. You get on to the carpet and make yourself comfortable. You are going to fly right away from here to somewhere much warmer. You are flying above towns and villages, field and farms. The houses and cars look unreal, like matchbox toys. Now you are over a beach and now the sea. At first the sea is grey but as we get to a warmer climate it gets bluer and bluer. You can feel the sun beating down on you.

Ahead you see a lush island with palm trees, white sand and clear blue sea. You land on the beach and look around for a minute or two breathing in the richly scented warm air. You take a stroll on the beach barefooted and feel the warmth of the sand on the soles of your feet. Dip your toes in the sea, it feels warm but refreshing.

Now walk into the jungle. There are beautiful exotic flowers everywhere - they smell wonderful and are clear bright colours - pinks, yellow, turquoise. High above you there are monkeys jumping from tree to tree chattering to each other and parrots flying around. Ahead you see a clearing in the jungle and walk towards it. There is a sleepy green lagoon bathed in green light from the sun passing through the tallest palm trees. On the lagoon is a little dinghy and you get into it and lie down.

You are bobbing gently in the lagoon in a pool of green light. You can hear the monkeys and birds screeching in the jungle but they sound a long way away.

You can smell the musky fragrance of the exotic flowers and fruit on the trees. Just enough sun can get through the trees to warm your body as you lie on the dinghy. Let yourself completely unwind as you relax breathing in the warmth and smells, hearing the sounds of the jungle.

When you are ready to come back, get up from the dinghy, walk slowly back through the jungle to your magic carpet. Make yourself comfortable on the carpet again ready for the journey home. You are flying back over the sea, then over land and now you can see your hometown. You land back where you started from and walk back into the room.

General Relaxation

This is a relaxation procedure that focuses on your muscles and how they feel. It uses the building up and letting go of muscle tension to help you learn to relax.

First of all you need to make yourself as comfortable as you can.

Take your time to do this now.

Ten seconds of silence.

As you sit or lie become aware of the sensations of the room around you. Notice any sounds you can hear. Notice the temperature of the air in your room and the feeling of your clothes. Just explore those sensations and become aware of them as you can and just enjoy any that feel particularly pleasant.

Ten seconds of silence.

To help you relax it is good to focus on simple sensations.

Ten seconds of silence

And now I would like you to focus on the feelings in your muscles. Just become aware of how your muscles are feeling. Either loose or tight, relaxed or tense or whatever. Just become aware of how they are feeling now.

20 seconds of silence.

And then I would like you to focus more on the muscles in your tummy. Become aware on how your tummy muscles are feeling. Just notice how you are holding those muscles.

Five seconds of silence.

And now I would like you to tense those muscles as much as you are able to.

Three seconds of silence.

Just notice how it feels to have them tense and hold them for a moment...

And now let go of the tension let the muscles relax. Notice how it feels to let go. Really notice the difference between the muscles being relaxed and them being tense.

Five seconds of silence.

Now I would like you to focus on the muscles in your back and chest. Become aware

Progressive Muscle Relaxation

Sit or lie down in a comfortable position. Relax yourself to the best of your ability.

Consider the various muscle groups one at a time, and aim to learn the difference between tight and relaxed muscles. Try constantly to concentrate on the feeling in the muscle as it goes from tight to loose.

Hands and arms.

Clench your fists, and tense your arms; feel tightness in your hands and arms, then slowly relax them.

See how far they will go, but do not push.

Do not hold on at all; let everything go.

Shoulders

Hunch your shoulders, then gradually let them settle down.

See how far they will go, but do not push.

Do not hold on at all; let everything go.

Forehead

Pull your eyebrows together, then gradually let your forehead smooth out.

Do not hold on at all; let everything go.

Eyes

Screw your eyes up tight, then gradually let them smooth out, leaving your eyes closed, feeling your eyeballs sink, and your eyelids droop.

Let them get really heavy.

Jaw

Bite your back teeth together, then gradually ease off, and let your jaw get heavy.

Back of neck

Pull your chin forward on to your chest, feel tightness, then relax.

Programme 4